A Short

Rabbi Professor Dan Cohn-Sherbok is a widely published and eminent scholar of Judaism. He is currently a lecturer at the University of Kent, Visiting Professor of Judaism at the University of Wales and Visiting Professor of Interfaith Dialogue at the University of Middlesex.

Lavinia Cohn-Sherbok taught Religious Studies for twenty years and until 1987 was Principal of West Heath School. She is now an honorary Research Fellow at the University of Kent, and is a writer specializing in Judaism and Jewish affairs.

Other books by Lavinia and Dan Cohn-Sherbok

The American Jew
A Popular Dictionary of Judaism
A Short History of Judaism

Other books by Dan Cohn-Sherbok

An Atlas of Jewish History
Blackwell Dictionary of Judaica
The Crucified Jew
Dictionary of Judaism and Christianity
The Jewish Faith
The Jewish Heritage
Jewish Mysticism: An Anthology
Judaism and Other Faiths
Holocaust Theology
Israel: The History of an Idea
Issues in Contemporary Judaism
The Future of Judaism

A Short Reader in Judaism

Compiled and edited by
Lavinia and Dan Cohn-Sherbok

ONEWORLD
OXFORD

A SHORT READER IN JUDAISM

Oneworld Publications
(Sales and Editorial)
185 Banbury Road
Oxford OX2 7AR
England

Oneworld Publications
(US Marketing Office)
PO Box 830, 21 Broadway
Rockport, MA 01966
USA

ISBN 1–85168–112–4

Printed and bound by
WSOY, Finland

Contents

Acknowledgements

'Zionism Condemned at UN', 'Israel Erupts' and 'Secret Air-Lift of Ethiopia's Jewish Community', reprinted with the permission of *The Times*. © Times Newspapers Limited, 1975/1982/1985

The Holocaust by Martin Gilbert, reprinted with the permission of HarperCollins Publishers Limited. Copyright © Martin Gilbert 1986

After Auschwitz by Richard L. Rubenstein, reprinted with the permission of Simon & Schuster, Inc. from the Macmillan College text. Copyright © Richard L. Rubenstein 1966

The Jewish Communities of the World, Antony Lerman, ed., reprinted with the permission of Macmillan Press Limited. Copyright © Antony Lerman 1989

Meaning of God in Modern Jewish Religion by Mordecai Kaplan, reprinted with the permission of Pantheon Books. Copyright © Mordecai Kaplan 1962

Tradition and Contemporary Experience, edited by A. Vospe, reprinted with the permission of Pantheon Books. Copyright © Mordecai Kaplan

The Second Jewish Catalog by Sharon and Michael Strassfeld, reprinted with the permission of the Jewish Publication Society. Copyright © Sharon and Michael Strassfeld 1983

The Collected Stories of Isaac Bashevis Singer by Isaac Bashevis Singer, reprinted with the permission of Jonathan Cape. Copyright © Isaac Bashevis Singer 1953

'Israel: The Years of Challenge' by David Ben-Gurion, reprinted with the permission of the *Spectator*.

Approaches to Auschwitz by Richard L. Rubenstein and John K. Roth, reprinted with the permission of SCM Press. Copyright © Richard L. Rubenstein 1987

One People? Tradition, Modernity, and Jewish Unity by Jonathan Sacks (London: The Littman Library of Jewish Civilization, 1993), reprinted with the permission of the Littman Library of Jewish Civilization.

Extracts from *Encyclopaedia Judaica* reprinted with the permission of Keter Publishing House Ltd.

'The San Francisco Platform, 1976' and 'Resolution of the Central Conference of American Rabbis' Copyright © 1977 and 1984 by the Central Conference of American Rabbis and reprinted with their permission.

Scroll of Agony: The Warsaw Diary of Chaim A. Kaplan, edited and translated by Abraham I. Katsh, reprinted with the permission of Simon & Schuster. Copyright © I. Katsh 1965

Tomorrow is Beautiful by Lucy R. Lang, reprinted with the permission of Simon & Schuster. Copyright © L.R. Lang 1948

To Heaven with the Scribes and Pharisees by Lionel Blue, reprinted with permission of Darton Longman & Todd.

The editors and publishers have made every effort to obtain permission from copyright holders. Apologies are offered if any existing copyrights have inadvertently been overlooked.

Preface

This reader is primarily intended to be used in conjunction with the authors' *A Short History of Judaism*. Although all the extracts are explained, they were chosen to illustrate the events described in the original volume. For ease of cross-reference, the chapter headings in both books are, with one exception, identical. All biblical quotations are from the RSV Bible; and all translations are the authors' own unless otherwise indicated.

Note on Abbreviations in Dates

Throughout this book the abbreviations BC (Before Christ) and AD (Anno Domini, In the Year of Our Lord) have been replaced with the more widely accepted BCE (Before Common, or Christian, Era) and CE (Common, or Christian, Era).

1

The Middle Eastern Background

1. Canaan and its Neighbours

The Jewish people believe themselves to be descended from Abraham (Abram), the leader of a Semitic tribe, who travelled throughout the land of Canaan:

> Now the Lord said to Abram, 'Go from your country and your kindred and your father's house to the land that I will show you. And I will make of you a great nation, and I will bless you, and make your name great, so that you will be a blessing. I will bless those who bless you, and him who curses you I will curse; and by you all the families of the earth shall bless themselves.'
>
> So Abram went, as the Lord had told him . . . And Abram took Sarai his wife and Lot his brother's son and all their possessions which they had gathered, and the persons that they had gotten in Haran; and they set forth to go to the land of Canaan. When they had come to the land of Canaan, Abram passed through the land to the place at Shechem, to the oak of Moreh. At that time the Canaanites were in the land. Then the Lord appeared to Abram and said, 'To your descendants will I give this land.' (Genesis 12: 1–7)

Later in the text Abraham's inheritance of the land of Canaan is made more explicit:

> Now Abram was very rich in cattle, in silver and in gold. And he journeyed on from the Negeb as far as Bethel, to the place where his tent had been at the beginning, between Bethel and Ai, to the place where he had made an altar at the first . . . The Lord said to Abram, after Lot had separated from him, 'Lift up your eyes and look from the place where you are, northward and southward and eastward and westward; for all the land which you see I will give to you and to your descendants for ever. I will make your descendants as the dust of the earth; so that if one can count the dust of the earth, your descendants also can be counted. Arise, walk through the length and breadth of the land, for I will give it to you.' So Abram moved his tent, and came and dwelt by the oaks of Mamre, which are at Hebron; and there he built an altar to the Lord. (Genesis 13: 2–3, 14–18)

Once the Israelites had settled in the land of Canaan after the Exodus from Egypt, their origins were remembered every year at the Ceremony of the First Fruits:

> When you come into the land which the Lord your God gives you for an inheritance, and have taken possession of it, and live in it, you shall take some of the first of all the fruit of the ground, which you harvest from your land that the Lord your God gives you, and you shall put it in a basket, and you shall go to the place which the Lord your God will choose to make his name to dwell there. And you shall go to the priest who is in office at that time, and say to him, 'I declare this day to the Lord your God that I have come into the land which the Lord swore to our fathers to give us.' Then the priest shall take the basket from your hand, and set it down before the altar of the Lord your God.
>
> And you shall make response before the Lord your God, 'A wandering Aramaean was my father.' (Deuteronomy 26: 1–5)

This folk memory of descent from a nomadic tribe is also retained in the book of Joshua:

> And Joshua said to all the people, 'Thus says the Lord, the God of Israel, "Your fathers lived of old beyond the Euphrates, Terah, the father of Abraham and of Nahor; and they served other gods. Then I took your father Abraham from beyond the river and led him through all the land of Canaan and made his offspring many."' (Joshua 24: 2–3)

The mode of life of the tribal nomads of this period is described in a Sumerian hymn:

> His arms are his companions . . .
> He never yields to his enemies,
> He eats his meat raw,
> Throughout his life he lives in no house,
> He leaves his dead comrade unburied.
>   (E. Chiera, 1924)

There is of course no firm evidence for the existence of the historical figure of Abraham except for the biblical text. There the land of Canaan itself is described as follows:

> On that day the Lord made a covenant with Abram, saying, 'To your descendants I give this land from the river of Egypt, to the great river, the River Euphrates, to the land of the Kenites, the Kenizzites, the Kadmonites, the

Hittites, the Perizzites, the Rephaim, the Amorites, the Canaanites, the Girgashites and the Jebusites.' (Genesis 15: 18–21)

Thus it stretched far further than the boundaries of the modern state of Israel. It extended from Egypt in the south, through Jordan in the east and deep into Syria in the north.

2. Archaeology of the Ancient Middle East

While Abraham and his descendants were nomads who spent their lives wandering through the desert, there is evidence of successful urban civilizations by the beginning of the second millennium BCE, and much of what we know of the beliefs and practices of the inhabitants of the ancient Middle East of this period is derived from archaeological excavation. For example, an immense archive of tablets has been found in Syria at Tel Mardikh, the ancient city of Ebla. These reflect the situation at the end of the third millennium, at least four hundred years before the time of the Patriarchs. They were excavated in 1975, but have not yet all been published because of the difficulty of the language. However, there are references to familiar biblical names such as Abraham (*Ab-ra-mu*), Esau (*E-sa-um*), Saul (*Sa-u-lum*), Israel (*Is-ra-ilu*), Eber (*Ib-num*) and David (*Da-u-dum*). Excavations at Mari on the River Euphrates have also produced a huge library of tablets including legal and economic documents. Examples of the tablets, which cast light on the biblical background, include:

> To my lord say: From Bannum your servant. I left Mari yesterday and passed the night at Zuruban. The Benjamites [Children of the South] were sending fire signals, but I have not yet understood their meaning . . . Strengthen the guard on the city of Mari. (G. Dossin, 1938)

> To my lord say . . . an armed column has gone out to raid the enemy forces, but since there was no base for attack, they have come back with nothing . . . I am sending Sakirum with three hundred soldiers to Shabazum . . . At the front of the troops will go Ilu-nazir, the prophet, one of my lord's subjects. (C. F. Jean, 1944)

> To my lord say . . . Sintiri sent to me for aid and I met him with troops at Shubat-Shamash. Next day there came news from the enemy saying, 'Yapah-Adad is defending Zallul on this side of the River Euphrates with two thousand soldiers of the Hapiru of the land.' (Ibid.)

Texts have also been discovered at Nuzu, to the east of the River Tigris, which date back to the fifteenth century BCE. Much has been made of the apparent similarity between the customs recorded in the tablets and customs described in the early books of the Bible:

> The tablet of adoption of Nashwi, the son of Arshenni: Nashwi adopted Wullu, son of Puhi-shenni. During Nashwi's lifetime, Wullu will provide food and clothing; at Nashwi's death, Wullu will inherit his property. If Nashwi has a son of his own, the estate will be divided equally with Wullu, but Nashwi's own son will take Nashwi's gods. If Nashwi has no son of his own, then Wullu will take Nashwi's gods. Nashwi gave Wullu his daughter Nuhuya to be his wife. If Wullu takes another wife, he will forfeit his inheritance from Nashwi. (C. J. Gudd, 1926)

This should be compared with Genesis 31: 17–50, where Jacob's wife Rachel steals her father's household gods for her husband and Jacob is warned to take no more wives.

> Tarmiya, the son of Huya, appeared against his two brothers Shukriya and Kula-hupi before the judges of Nuzu in a legal suit concerning a female slave . . . The witnesses were examined . . . then the judges told Shukriya and Kula-hupi to take the oath of the gods against Tarmiya's witness. They shrank from taking the gods' oath so Tarmiya prevailed in the law suit. (E. A. Speiser, 1936. This might be compared with the Ordeal of Bitter Waters undergone by women accused of unfaithfulness as described in Numbers 5: 16–28.)

Tablets dating from the early fourteenth century BCE have also been found at Tell el-Amarna on the River Nile in Egypt. They reflect the situation in Palestine before the supposed date of the Jews' Exodus when Canaan was part of the Egyptian empire. Examples include:

> From 'Abdi-tirshi, the Ruler of Hazor, to the King of Egypt. He rejoices in receiving a message from the King his master and he promises that he will guard and protect the king's cities.
> From Yapahi, the Ruler of Gezer, to the King of Egypt. The writer acknowledges the King's letter and asks for further help against the Habiru.
> From Widiya, Governor of Ashkelon, to the King of Egypt. He reports that he is fulfilling his responsibilities in guarding the cities. He has prepared the promised tribute for the King.
> From Yahtiri, Governor of Gaza and Joppa, to the King of Egypt. The writer declares his loyalty to the King and reminds him that he was brought up in Egypt at the King's court.
> From Shipti-baal of Lachish to the King of Egypt. The writer assures the King of his loyalty and fidelity and that of Yanhamu.
> From Shuwardata, Prince of Hebron, to the King of Egypt. He reports

that he has been left without resources and that he is in immediate need of reinforcements if he is to be saved. (Letters 47, 49, 52, 57, 65 and 68, Tell el-Amarna Letters [British Museum numbering])

3. Law in Mesopotamia and Babylon

The legal codes and treaties of Ancient Babylon and Mesopotamia show clear similarities to the laws and customs of the Jews. The earliest discovered code dates from 2050 BCE. It was drawn up by Ur Nammu, King of Sumer and Akkad. Provisions include:

If a man has accused another man . . . and brought him to the river-ordeal, if the river-ordeal proves him innocent, the accuser must pay him three shekels of silver. (Text A, lines 270–80)
　　If a man severed the foot of another, he must pay ten shekels of silver. (Lines 324–30)
　　If a man acts as a witness and is shown to perjure himself, he must pay fifteen shekels of silver. (Text B, line 34) (S. N. Kramer, 1954)

Another collection, found near Baghdad, came from the ancient kingdom of Eshunna. It dates from *c.* 1920 BCE:

If a man bites another man's nose and cuts it off, he shall pay one minna of silver, for an eye one minna of silver, for a tooth half a minna and for an ear half a minna.
　　If an ox is known regularly to gore and the owner has been told by the authorities, but has not removed its horns, if the ox gores a man to death then the owner of the ox shall pay two thirds of a minna of silver. (Paragraphs 46 and 54, Iraq Museum 51059 and 52614)

The Code of King Hammurabi of Babylon dates from the late eighteenth century BCE. After a long introduction, citing the King's commission to legislate from the god Marduk, provisions include:

If a free citizen accuses a fellow citizen of murder, but does not prove the charge, the accuser shall be put to death.
　　If a free citizen sells his wife, his son or his daughter to repay a debt, they shall work for three years in the house of their master, but in the fourth year they shall be freed.
　　If a citizen has given another citizen silver or gold for safe-keeping in the presence of witnesses and he later denies it, that citizen shall restore the valuables twice over.
　　If a free citizen has handed any of his possessions for safe-keeping and if

the place where it was deposited is broken into and the property is lost, the householder who has been neglectful shall make restitution of everything that was lost to the owner and will search thoroughly for the lost items to get them back from the thief.

If a son strikes his father, his hand shall be cut off.

If a free citizen destroys the eye of another free citizen, his eye will be destroyed.

If an ox gored a free citizen and caused him to die, no penalty is payable.

If, however, the ox has the propensity to gore and its owner has not removed its horns or tethered it and it gores a free citizen to death, the owner will pay half a minna of silver. (Paragraphs 1, 123–5, 195, 196, 250 and 251, V. Scheil, 1902)

The oldest Jewish law code, the so-called Book of the Covenant, is to be found in Exodus 20: 22–23: 33. It shares many similarities with the earlier codes:

And the Lord said to Moses, 'Thus you shall say to the people of Israel: "You have seen for yourselves that I have talked with you from Heaven . . . When you buy a Hebrew slave, he shall serve six years and in the seventh he shall go out free for nothing . . . Whoever strikes his father or his mother shall be put to death . . . You shall give life for life, eye for eye, tooth for tooth, hand for hand, foot for foot . . . When an ox gores a man or a woman to death, the ox shall be stoned . . . but the owner of the ox shall be cleared. But if the ox is accustomed to gore in the past, and its owner has been warned, but has not kept it in and it kills a man or a woman, the ox shall be stoned and its owner shall also be put to death . . . If a man delivers to his neighbour money or goods to keep, and it is stolen out of the man's house, then if the thief is found, he shall pay double. If the thief is not found, the owner of the house shall come near to God, to show whether or not he has put his hand to his neighbour's goods." ' (Exodus 20: 22; 21: 2, 15, 23, 24, 28, 29; 22: 7, 8 and 23: 1)

Similarities can also be found between formulations of Israelite law and those of Hittite and Assyrian treaties between king and vassal. These treaties date back to the end of the second millennium BCE. For example, in the treaty between Mursilis, King of the Hittites and his vassal Duppi-Tessub of the Amurru, the King describes the historical background to the treaty. He then goes on:

After I found you, in obedience to your father's instructions, and put you in his place, I, as King of the Hittites, made an oath with you, for me and for my son and for my grandson. Keep this oath of loyalty to your King and to his family! And I, as King, will be faithful to you, Duppi-Tessub. When you marry and have a son, he will also be King of the Amurru in his turn. And just as I am faithful to you, I will be faithful to your son. But you must remain faithful to the King of the Hittites and towards his descendants for ever. Your grandfather and father paid tribute – three hundred shekels of good refined gold measured out – and you must pay tribute as well. Do not look to anyone else. (E. F. Weidner, 1923)

This might be compared with:

And when the Lord your God brings you into the land which he swore to your fathers, to Abraham, to Isaac and to Jacob . . . then take heed lest you forget the Lord . . . You shall fear the Lord your God, you shall serve him and swear by his name. You shall not go after other gods. (Deuteronomy 6: 10–14)

4. Ancient Middle Eastern Religion

Also from archaeological excavation, we know a great deal about the religions of the ancient Middle East. As the following extracts will show, there are clear similarities with early biblical ideas. The Babylonians had their own version of the Creation story, which they recited every year at their New Year festival. This version dates back to approximately the sixteenth century BCE.

Before the creation of the gods of Heaven and before the gods of the earth had come into existence, there lived only Apsu, the ancient ocean, who begat them, with Mummu and Tiamat who gave them birth. All their waters could flow together in one rush with no marshes or reeds to impede them. None of the other gods had yet come into existence. As yet they had no shape or determined destinies. It was in the waters that the gods were created; first appeared Lahmu and Lahamu who received their names; they only grew to a certain size and Anshar and Kishar were larger than they at their birth. As time went on and the years passed, Anshar produced his first-born son Anu. Anu was like his parents and he was the father of Ea, who was made in his own likeness. Yet Ea, Nudimmud, was greater than his father, more intelligent, wiser and stronger. He was greater too than his grandfather Anshar, and none of the other gods, his brothers, could match up to him. (George Smith, 1876)

The saga goes on to describe how Apsu cannot bear the noise generated by the new gods and resolves to destroy them. Ea, however, casts a spell over Apsu and, while he is asleep, kills him. Apsu's wife, Tiamat, decides to revenge her husband. Both Ea and Anu are forced to retreat against her, but Ea's son, Marduk, takes on the role of supreme champion of the gods:

> And so Marduk and Tiamat met together. They advanced against one another in battle. The Lord Marduk spread out his net and covered her while the Evil Wind blew in her face behind. She was about to open her mouth to consume him, but he sent the Evil Wind into her mouth. Her insides were filled with the furious raging of the storm and her belly became distended while her mouth was wide open. Then Marduk shot her with an arrow. It pierced her stomach, it shot through her bowels and ripped into her womb. Then he strangled her so that she could no longer breathe. He threw her body onto the earth and stood over her in triumph. (Ibid.)

After the battle Marduk divided her body into two to form the sky and the earth and he was acknowledged by his fellow gods to be their king.

Like the Jews, the ancient Babylonians also had a tale of a great flood. It is generally known as the Epic of Gilgamesh and is based on earlier Sumerian stories. This version dates back to the late eighteenth century BCE:

> Utnapishti spoke to Gilgamesh, 'Gilgamesh, I will tell you of a secret matter, a hidden secret of the gods. The city of Shuruppak which you know, which lies on the banks of the Euphrates and which is now in ruins – when that city was still old and still had gods living within its walls, the great gods decided to send down a flood.' (Ibid.)

The building of a great boat is described and Utnapishti explains how it was loaded and closed:

> At the time of the dawn a great cloud came up out of the horizon. Adad [the storm God] was in thunder within it; Shullat and Hanish [other gods] led the way, going out with their followers over plain and mountain. Nergal ripped out the irrigation dams that they found and the dam walls. Ninurta followed and caused the weirs to overflow. The Anunnaki had lit their torches in order to cast light over the land, but as the Black Cloud of Adad passed across the skies, the light was turned into deepest darkness. The cloud blew swiftly . . . it went over the earth like a battle. A man could not recognize his own brother and people could not even be seen from the Heavens. The gods themselves were terrified of the flood; they fled to the Heaven of Anu; they shook like dogs and crouched in hiding by the outside walls . . . The wind raged for six days and seven nights and the storm and the flood swept over the land. On the seventh day, the storm was hushed and the flood which had heaved like a woman in labour was quieted. The sea was calm

and the wind of the storm stopped blowing and the flood stood still. I opened a hatch and the fresh air blew on my cheeks. I looked over the sea; there was a silence and the tide was as flat as a roof tile – but all of humanity had returned to the clay . . . After seven more days I released a dove from the great ship. He flew out, but he came back because there was no place for him to rest. I also released a sparrow. He flew out, but he came back because there was no place for him to rest. Then I released a raven. Out he went and he saw the natural flow of the waters. He ate, he fluttered about, he croaked, and he did not come back to me. (Ibid.)

The story ends with Utnapishti being given immortality by the gods.

The discovery of the Ras Shamra tablets at Ugarit in 1928 has added a great deal to our knowledge of the religion of the ancient peoples of Canaan. Their chief god, Baal, is mentioned in the Bible and the Ras Shamra texts dating from the late fourteenth century BCE give us tantalizing glimpses of his adventures:

What enemy can stand against Baal? Who will oppose the one who climbs upon the clouds? I killed Sea, the dear one of El [the creator god], I destroyed the great god River. I subdued the Dragon and held her in bonds. I slaughtered the crooked serpent, the evil-mouthed one with the seven heads. I have killed those whom the earth gods love. Death, who goes by with huge haste I have overcome. I have slaughtered Fire, the bitch of the gods. I have destroyed Flame, the daughter of El and I have beaten and exiled the Flood who wished to drive Baal from the mountains of Saphon.

El, the merciful and compassionate, had a dream. The creator of all Creation had a vision. Oil rained from Heaven. Honey flowed from the wadis. El, the compassionate and merciful rejoices. He sits with his feet on a foot-stool, he relaxes and he laughs. He lifts up his voice and declares, 'I shall sit and relax and I shall rest my soul, for the mighty Baal is alive. Baal exists as Prince and Lord of the earth.' (C. F. A. Schaeffer, 1939).

5. The Emergence of the Jews

The Jews trace their descent from the 'wandering Aramaean', Abraham, through the Patriarchs Isaac and Jacob and through Jacob's twelve sons who settled in Egypt. This understanding was enshrined in the liturgy:

A wandering Aramaean was my father; and he went down into Egypt and sojourned there, few in number; and there he became a nation, great, mighty and populous. And the Egyptians treated us harshly and afflicted us, and laid upon us hard bondage. Then we cried to the Lord, the God of our fathers, and the Lord heard our voice, and saw our affliction, our toil and our oppression, and the Lord brought us out of Egypt, with a mighty hand and an outstretched arm, with great terror, with signs and wonders; and he brought us into this place and gave us this land flowing with milk and honey. (Deuteronomy 26: 5–9)

The archaeological evidence neither confirms nor denies this account. The Mari and Nuzu texts (see Chapter 1, Part 2) as well as the Tell el-Amarna letters mention the existence of the 'Apiru:

To my Lord the King, my Sun God, say: thus says your servant Abdik-eba. At the King's feet, my lord, do I fall seven times seven . . . Let the King take advice for the land. The King's land is lost; all of it has been taken away from me. There is enmity towards me as far away as the lands of Seir and Gath-carmel. Although there is peace towards all the regents, there is enmity towards me. I am treated like an 'Apiru and because there is enmity towards me I do not see the eyes of the King my lord. They have made me like a ship in the middle of the sea. The might of the King may capture Naharaim and Cush, but now the 'Apiru have captured the King's cities. The King my lord has no regents left; they are all lost. (Letter 288, J. A. Knudtzon, 1907–15)

The relationship of the 'Apiru and the Israelites, however, is the subject of much scholarly debate. It is now generally accepted that the two groups were related, but were not identical (see Roland de Vaux, *The Early History of Israel*, pp. 209–16).

Similarly there have been attempts to identify the Pharaoh who welcomed Jacob and his sons into Egypt with a member of the Hyksos dynasty of the seventeenth and sixteenth centuries BCE. Although the evidence is scanty, we know that the Hyksos were of Asiatic extraction. Their Pharaohs lived in the city of Avaris on the eastern delta of the Nile and they called themselves 'the rulers of the foreign land'. It has been argued that such kings would have welcomed Asiatic nomads such as Jacob and his sons. We do know that the Egyptians themselves rejoiced at the expulsion of the Hyksos. This inscription of Queen Hatshepsut gives a flavour of the hatred of this dynasty:

Hear all you people, as many as there are. I have done these many things. I have not forgotten or slept, but I have restored all that was overthrown. I have reconstructed what was thrown down in the days of the Asiatics of Avaris or the Northland, when nomads were among us destroying everything around them. They reigned without Re [the sun god] and their

Pharaoh acted without the divine command. But now I sit upon the throne of Re. It was prophesied that I was born to conquer. (W. Golenischeff, 1885)

Some scholars do believe that the Hyksos deposition in the middle of the sixteenth century BCE is reflected in the situation recorded in the book of Exodus:

Now there arose a new king over Egypt, who did not know Joseph. And he said to his people, 'Behold the people of Israel are too many and too mighty for us. Come, let us deal shrewdly with them, lest they multiply, and, if war befall us, they join our enemies and fight against us and escape from the land.' Therefore they set taskmasters over them to afflict them with heavy burdens; and they built for Pharaoh store-cities, Pithom and Raamses. But the more they were oppressed, the more they multiplied and the more they spread abroad. And the Egyptians were in dread of the people of Israel. So they made the people of Israel serve with rigour, and made their lives bitter with hard service in mortar and brick, and in all kinds of work in the field; in all their work they made them serve with rigour. (Exodus 1: 8–14)

Again, however, this is generally felt to be too tidy a solution (see Roland de Vaux, *The Early History of Israel*, pp. 318–20).

Chronological Table

Circa BCE	Documents	Events in Jewish History
2400–2200	Tel Mardikh tablets	
2200–2000	Ur Nammu's legal code; Sumerian hymn	
2000–1800	Mari tablets; Eshunna legal code	Age of the Patriarchs c. 1900–1600
1800–1600	King Hammurabi's legal code; Babylonian Creation epic; Queen Hatshepsut's inscription	
1400–1200	Ras Shamra texts; Treaty between Mursilis and Duppi-Tessub	Era of the Exodus c. 1400–1200
1200–1000	Book of the Covenant	

Suggested Further Reading

The books of Genesis and Exodus.

R. de Vaux, *The Early History of Israel to the Period of the Judges*, London: Darton, Longman & Todd, 1978.

J. B. Pritchard, ed., *Ancient Near Eastern Texts* (3rd edn.) Princeton, NJ: Princeton University Press, 1969.

D. Winton Thomas, ed., *Documents from Old Testament Times*, New York: Harper Collins Publishers, 1961.

2

The Pentateuch

1. The Status of the Pentateuch in Jewish Theology

The traditional view is that the Pentateuch (the biblical books of Genesis, Exodus, Leviticus, Numbers and Deuteronomy) was given to Moses directly by God:

> Miriam and Aaron spoke against Moses because of the Cushite woman whom he had married, for he had married a Cushite woman; and they said, 'Has the Lord indeed spoken only through Moses? Has he not spoken through us also?' And the Lord heard it. Now the man Moses was very meek, more than all men that were on the face of the earth. And suddenly the Lord said to Moses and to Aaron and Miriam, 'Come out, you three, to the tent of meeting.' And the three of them came out. And the Lord came down in a pillar of cloud, and stood at the door of the tent, and called Aaron and Miriam; and they both came forward. And he said, 'Hear my words; if there is a prophet among you, I the Lord make myself known to him in a vision, I speak with him in a dream. Not so with my servant Moses; he is entrusted with all my house. With him I speak mouth to mouth, clearly, and not in dark speech; and he beholds the form of the Lord. Why then were you not afraid to speak against my servant Moses?' (Numbers 12: 1–8)

> And there has not arisen a prophet since in Israel like Moses, whom the Lord knew face to face, none like him for all the signs and the wonders which the Lord sent him to do in the Land of Egypt, to Pharaoh and to all his servants and to all his land, and for all the mighty power and all the great and terrible deeds which Moses wrought in the sight of all Israel. (Deuteronomy 34: 10–11)

The conviction that Moses was the mouthpiece of God and the author of the Pentateuch is enshrined in Jewish thought. For example, the twelfth-century philosopher Moses Maimonides formulated it as his seventh, eighth and ninth principles of the Jewish faith:

7. I believe with perfect faith that the prophecy of Moses our teacher (may everlasting peace be with him!) is true; and that he was chief of all the prophets who preceded him and of all who succeeded him.

8. I believe with perfect faith that the whole and complete Law as we now have it, is one and the same as that given to Moses (may everlasting peace be with him!).

9. I believe with perfect faith that the Law will never be changed, nor that any other law will be given in its place by the Creator (blessed be His name!).
(Moses Maimonides, Principles of the Jewish Faith, Ashkenazi Prayer Book)

The Yigdal, a well-known hymn based on Maimonides' Principles, is still sung regularly in the synagogue:

> The gift of prophecy He did consign
> Unto a chosen few of glorious line;
> But like to Moses none in Israel rose,
> Before whose gaze Himself did God disclose.
> The Law of Truth He hath His people given,
> The prophet always proved most true to Heaven;
> God's law will stand as long as time will be,
> Changeless still through all eternity.
> (Ashkenazi Prayer Book)

In the liturgical services, the reverence in which the Pentateuch is held is illustrated in the following benedictions:

> Blessed be He who gave the Law to His people Israel in His Holiness; the Law of the Lord is perfect, refreshing the soul; the Testimony of the Lord is lasting, making the simple wise; the Rules of the Lord are just, rejoicing the heart; the Commandments of the Lord are clear, enlightening the eyes; the Lord will give strength to His people; the Lord will bless His people with peace . . .
>
> Blessed are you, O Lord our God, King of the Universe, who has chosen us from all the people and has given us His Law. Blessed are you O Lord, who has given us the Law . . .
>
> And this is the Law which Moses put before the children of Israel, as commanded by the Lord, through the hand of Moses; it is the tree of life to those who grasp it and those who hold it are truly happy; its ways are ways of pleasantness and all its paths are peace. (Order for reading the Law in the Ashkenazi Prayer Book)

Orthodox Jews continue to maintain that God gave the whole Pentateuch to Moses as an article of faith:

Let us not deceive ourselves. The whole question is simply this. Is the statement, 'And God spoke to Moses saying . . .' with which all the laws of the Jewish Bible commence, true or not true? Do we really believe that God, the Omnipotent and Holy, spoke thus to Moses? Do we speak the truth when in front of our brethren we lay our hand on the scroll containing these words and say that God has given us this Torah, that His Torah, the Torah of truth and with it of eternal life, is planted in our midst? If this is to be no mere lip service, no mere rhetorical flourish, then we must keep and carry out this Torah without omission and without carping, in all circumstances and at all times. This Word of God must be our eternal rule superior to all human judgement, the rule to which all our actions must at all times conform; and instead of complaining it is no longer suitable to the time, our only complaint must be that the times are no longer suitable to it. (Samson Raphael Hirsch, *Judaism Eternal*)

2. The Authorship of the Pentateuch

As early as the seventeenth century, the heretical philosopher Spinoza (see Chapter 10, Part 2) had called into question the Mosaic authorship of the Pentateuch:

First I shall discuss misconceptions regarding the true authorship of the Sacred Books starting with the Pentateuch. Moses is almost universally believed to be the author and this view is held so rigidly by the Pharisees that they have castigated any other opinion as heresy. Because of this ibn Ezra, a most learned and enlightened man, who was, as far as I know, the first to call attention to this misconception, did not try to explain his meaning openly . . . [but] he gives a clear indication that it was not Moses who wrote the Pentateuch, but someone who lived long after him . . .

We may therefore conclude that the Book of the Law of God written by Moses was not the Pentateuch, but a different book . . . and this conclusion is based on very clear evidence . . . In the passage of Deuteronomy . . . which tells us that Moses wrote the Book of the Law, the writer adds that Moses delivered it into the hands of the priests and furthermore that he ordered them to read it out to the assembled people at the appointed time. This must mean that the book in question was much shorter than the Pentateuch, as it could be read and understood by all in a single meeting . . . Since then there is no evidence that Moses wrote any other books and, finally, since there are many passages in the Pentateuch which could not have been written by Moses, it follows that there are no grounds for believing Moses to be the author of the Pentateuch. (Baruch Spinoza, *Tractatus Theologico-Politicus*)

In contrast to the Orthodox, the progressive denominations within

Judaism (see Chapter 10, Part 3) always welcomed the findings of biblical criticism:

> The treatment of the historical account of the Bible as part of the science of Judaism must be subject to all laws which may be termed the science of history. The authenticity of the sources must be investigated, their genuineness and reliability must be studied, and it must be seen whether the sources give us a complete rendition of reality or whether they enclose it – in accordance with a certain outlook which we must understand – in a husk, the kernel of which we must liberate. No dogmatic presuppositions must interfere with the methods of such scientific criticism. (Abraham Geiger, *Das Judenthum und Seine Geschichte*)

The idea that the Pentateuch draws on earlier written sources was popularized in the scholarly world by Julius Wellhausen in the late nineteenth century:

> For the Law, if by this we understand the whole Pentateuch, is not a literary unity nor a single historical survey. Since the time of Peyrerius and Spinoza, the complex character of this remarkable literary production has been acknowledged and critics from Jean Anstruc onwards have laboured at disentangling its original elements with some success. At present there are several conclusions which we can regard as definite. The following include: the five books of Moses and the book of Joshua constitute one whole, so the conquest of the Promised Land rather than the death of Moses forms the true conclusion to the stories of the Patriarchs, the Exodus and the wanderings in the wilderness. From a literary viewpoint, then, it is more accurate to speak of the Hexateuch than the Pentateuch. From this, the book of Deuteronomy, which is essentially an independent law book, can be most easily separated. Of the remaining texts, the parts most easily distinguished belong to the so-called 'ground material', formerly called the Elohist Document, on account of the use it makes of the divine name Elohim up to the time of Moses . . . It is distinguished by its liking for number and measure and formulae generally, by its stiff pedantic style and by its constant use of certain phrases and turns of expression which do not occur elsewhere in the older Hebrew . . . When this fundamental document is also separated out as well as Deuteronomy, there remains the Jehovistic history book which, in contrast with the other sources, is essentially of a narrative character and sets forth with full sympathy and enjoyment the materials handed down by tradition . . . Scholars for a long time remained satisfied with the two-fold division of the non-Deuteronomic Hexateuch, until Hupfeld demonstrated in a certain part of Genesis . . . the existence of a third continuous sources. (Julius Wellhausen, *Prolegomena der Geschichte Israels*)

Wellhausen himself saw that the sources of the Pentateuch were likely to be more complex than this:

> The fact is coming to be more and more clearly perceived, that not only the Jehovistic document, but the 'ground material' also are complex products, and that alongside them occur hybrids of posthumous elements which do not admit of being simply referred to in either the one or the other formation. (Ibid.)

Although the precise boundaries of the different sources of the Pentateuch are still much disputed by scholars, Wellhausen's documentary hypothesis remains helpful when tracing the early history of the Jewish people.

3. The JE Sources

In the story of the Jews' Exodus from Egypt, the narratives of the J source have been skilfully woven together. From the J source we read:

> The Lord [JHWH] said to Moses, 'Tell the people of Israel to turn back and encamp in front of Piha-hiroth, between Migdol and the sea, in front of Baal-zephon; you shall encamp over against it, by the sea.'
> The minds of Pharaoh and his servants were changed towards the people, and they said, 'What is this we have done, that we have let Israel go from serving us?' So he made ready his chariot and took six hundred picked chariots.
> The Egyptians pursued them, and overtook them encamped at the sea, by Piha-hiroth, in front of Baal-zephon. When Pharaoh drew near, the people of Israel lifted up their eyes, and behold the Egyptians were marching after them; and they were in great fear. And the people of Israel cried out to the Lord.
> And Moses said to the people, 'Fear not, stand firm, and see the salvation of the Lord which he will work for you today; for the Egyptians whom you see today, you shall never see again. The Lord will fight for you, and you have only to be still.'
> And the pillar of cloud moved from before them and stood behind them, coming between the host of Egypt and the host of Israel. There was the cloud and the darkness and the night passed; and the Lord drove the sea back by a strong east wind all night and made the sea dry land. (Exodus 14: 2, 5b–7a, 9a, 9c–10, 13–14, 19b–20b, 21b)

From the E source we read:

> When Pharaoh let the people go, God [Elohim] did not lead them by way of the land of the Philistines, although that was near; for God said, 'Lest the

people repent when they see war, and return to Egypt.' But God led the people round by the way of the wilderness towards the Red Sea. And the people of Israel went up out of the land of Egypt equipped for battle. And Moses took the bones of Joseph with him; for Joseph had solemnly sworn to the people of Israel saying, 'God will visit you, then you must carry my bones with you from here.'

When the King of Egypt was told that the people had fled, he took his army with him and all the other chariots of Egypt with officers over all of them, all Pharaoh's horses and chariots, his horsemen and his army. And they [the people] said to Moses, 'Is it because there are no graves in Egypt that you have taken us away to die in the wilderness? Is not this what we said to you in Egypt, "Leave us alone and let us serve the Egyptians." For it would have been better for us to serve the Egyptians than to die in the wilderness.'

Then the angel of God who went before the host of Israel moved and went behind them; and the night passed without one coming near the other all night. (Exodus 3: 17–19; 14: 5a, 6b, 7b, 9b, 11–12, 19a, 20c)

The two sources do not agree on such matters as when human beings first called the Lord by his name. According to the J source:

To Seth [son of Adam] also a son was born and he called his name Enosh. At that time men began to call upon the name of the Lord [JHWH]. (Genesis 4: 26)

According to the E source:

And God [Elohim] said to Moses, 'I am the Lord [JHWH]. I appeared to Abraham, to Isaac and to Jacob as God Almighty [El Shaddai], but by my name the Lord [JHWH] I did not make myself known to them.' (Exodus 6: 2–3)

It is generally believed that the J source originated in the south among the tribe of Judah, while the E source came from the north, from the tribe of Reuben. This is illustrated in their different versions of the Joseph story. According to the J source:

Judah said to his brothers, 'What profit is it if we slay our brother and conceal his blood? Come let us sell him to the Ishmaelites, and let not our hand be upon him, for he is our brother, our own flesh.' And his brothers heeded him and sold him to the Ishmaelites for twenty shekels of silver. (Genesis 37: 26, 27, 28b)

In the E version it is Reuben who saves Joseph:

But when Reuben heard it he delivered him out of their hands, saying, 'Let us not take his life.' And Reuben said to them, 'Shed no blood; cast him into this pit here in the wilderness, but lay no hand upon him' – that he might rescue him out of their hand, to restore him to his father. So when Joseph came to his brothers, they stripped him of his robe, the long robe with sleeves that he wore; and they took him and cast him into a pit. The pit was empty, there was no water in it. Then Midianite traders passed by; and they drew Joseph up and lifted him out of the pit. When Reuben returned to the pit and saw that Joseph was not in the pit, he rent his clothes and returned to his brothers and said, 'The lad is gone; and I, where shall I go?' (Genesis 37: 21–4, 28a, 29–30)

Supporters of the documentary hypothesis believe that the J source and the E source were combined together after the fall of Samaria in 721 BCE (see Chapter 3, Part 4). The present text of the Pentateuch consists of this redaction, which includes the story of the creation of humanity:

In the day that the Lord God made the earth and the heavens when no plant of the field was yet in the earth and no herb of the field had yet sprung up – for the Lord God had not caused it to rain upon the earth, and there was no man to till the ground; but a mist went up from the earth and watered the whole face of the ground – then the Lord God formed man of dust from the ground, and breathed into his nostrils the breath of life; and man became a living being. And the Lord God planted a garden in Eden, in the east, and there he put the man whom he had formed. And out of the ground the Lord God made to grow every tree that is pleasant to the sight and good for food . . . Then the Lord God said, 'It is not good that the man should be alone; I will make a helper fit for him.' So out of the ground the Lord God formed every beast of the field and every bird of the air, and brought them to the man . . . but for the man there was not found a helper fit for him. So the Lord God caused a deep sleep to fall upon the man, and while he slept took one of his ribs and closed up its place with flesh; and the rib which the Lord God had taken from the man he made into a woman and brought her to the man. (Genesis 2: 4b–9a, 18–19b, 21–2)

4. The D Source

Most scholars believe that the core of the D source was associated with the law book found in the Temple in the reign of Josiah (see Chapter 3, Part 5):

And Hilkiah the high priest said to Shaphan the secretary, 'I have found the book of the law in the house of the Lord.' And Hilkiah gave the book to

Shaphan and he read it. And Shaphan the secretary came to the King and reported to the King, 'Your servants have emptied out the money that was found in the house, and have delivered it into the hand of the workmen who have the oversight of the house of the Lord.' Then Shaphan the secretary told the King, 'Hilkiah has given me a book.' And Shaphan read it before the King.

And when the King heard the words of the book of the law, he rent his clothes. And the King commanded Hilkiah the priest and Ahikam the son of Shaphan, and Achbor the son of Micaiah and Shaphan the secretary and Asaiah the King's servant, saying, 'Go, inquire of the Lord for me, and for the people, and for all Judah, concerning the words of this book that has been found; for great is the wrath of the Lord that is kindled against us, because our fathers have not obeyed the words of this book, to do according to all that is written concerning us.' (II Kings 22: 8–13)

The D writer believed that the key to the Jewish people's survival lay in obedience to the commandments of God:

See, I have set before you this day life and good, death and evil. If you obey the commandments of the Lord your God which I command you this day, by loving the Lord your God, by walking in his ways and by keeping his commandments and his statutes and his ordinances, then you shall live and multiply, and the Lord your God will bless you in the land which you are entering to take possession of it. But if your heart turns away, and you will not hear, but are drawn away to worship other gods and serve them, I declare to you this day, that you shall perish; you shall not live long in the land which you are going over the Jordan to enter and possess. I call heaven and earth to witness against you this day, that I have set before you life and death, blessing and curse. (Deuteronomy 30: 15–19)

Many of the Deuteronomic laws are concerned with correct behaviour towards others:

You shall not give up to his master a slave who has escaped from his master to you; he shall dwell with you in your midst in the place which he shall choose within one of your towns, where it pleases him best; you shall not oppress him.

When a man is newly married, he shall not go out with the army or be charged with any business; he shall be free at home one year, to be happy with his wife whom he has taken.

You shall not pervert the justice due to the sojourner or to the fatherless, or take a widow's garment in pledge; but you shall remember that you were a slave in Egypt and the Lord your God redeemed you from there; therefore I command you to do this.

When you go into your neighbour's vineyard, you may eat your fill of grapes, as many as you wish, but you shall not put any in your vessel. When you go into your neighbour's standing grain, you may pluck the ears with your hand, but you shall not put a sickle to your neighbour's standing grain. (Deuteronomy 23: 15–16; 24: 5, 17–18, 23: 24–5)

There are also instructions on correct ritual practice and the writer is emphatic that any sacrifice to God may only be performed at one central sanctuary:

Observe the month of Abib, and keep the Passover to the Lord your God; for in the month of Abib the Lord your God brought you out of Egypt by night. And you shall offer the Passover sacrifice to the Lord your God from the flock or the herd, at the place which the Lord will choose to make his name dwell there. You shall eat no leavened bread with it; seven days you shall eat it with unleavened bread, the bread of affliction – for you came out of the land of Egypt in hurried flight . . .

You shall count seven weeks; begin to count the seven weeks from the time you first put the sickle to the standing grain. Then you shall keep the feast of weeks to the Lord your God with the tribute of a freewill offering from your hand, which you shall give as the Lord your God blesses you . . .

You shall keep the feast of booths seven days, when you make your ingathering from your threshing floor and your wine press; you shall rejoice in your feast, you and your son and your daughter, your manservant and your maidservant, the Levite, the sojourner, the fatherless and the widow who are within your towns . . .

Three times a year all your males shall appear before the Lord your God at the place where he will choose, at the feast of unleavened bread, at the feast of weeks and at the feast of booths. (Deuteronomy 16: 1–3, 9–10, 13–14, 16)

The book ends with the death of Moses:

And Moses went up from the plains of Moab to Mount Nebo, to the top of Pisgah, which is opposite Jericho. And the Lord showed him all the land, Gilead as far as Dan, all Naphtali, the land of Ephraim and Manasseh, all the land of Judah as far as the Western Sea, the Negeb, and the plain, that is, the valley of Jericho, the city of palm trees, as far as Zoar. And the Lord said to him, 'This is the land of which I swore to Abraham, to Isaac and to Jacob "I will give it to your descendants." I have let you see it with your eyes, but you shall not go over there.' So Moses the servant of the Lord died there in the land of Moab, according to the word of the Lord, and he buried him in the valley in the land of Moab opposite Beth-peor; but no man knows the place of his burial to this day. (Deuteronomy 34: 1–6)

5. The P Source

The fourth source of the Pentateuch is known as P because it is thought that its author came from a priestly background. The Holiness Code in Leviticus (Chapters 17–26) in particular, is ascribed to him:

> And the Lord said to Moses, 'Say to all the congregation of the people of Israel, "You shall be holy; for I the Lord your God am holy. Every one of you shall revere his mother and his father and you shall keep my sabbaths; I am the Lord your God. Do not turn to idols or make for yourselves molten gods; I am the Lord your God."' (Leviticus 19: 1–4)

> I am the Lord your God, who have separated you from the peoples. You shall therefore make a distinction between the clean beast and the unclean, and between the unclean bird and the clean; you shall not make yourself abominable by beast or by bird or by anything with which the ground teems, which I have set apart for you to hold unclean. You shall be holy to me; for I the Lord am holy, and have separated you from the peoples, that you should be mine. (Leviticus 20: 24b–6)

The P source gives extensive regulations for the sons of Aaron, the priestly caste:

> And the Lord said to Moses, 'Speak to the priests, the sons of Aaron, and say to them that none of them shall defile himself for the dead among his people except for his nearest of kin . . . He shall not defile himself as a husband among his people and so profane himself. They shall not make tonsures upon their heads nor shave off the edges of their beards, nor make any cuttings in their flesh. They shall be holy to their God, and not profane the name of their God; for they offer the offerings by fire to the Lord, the bread of their God; therefore they shall be holy. They shall not marry a harlot or a woman who has been defiled; neither shall they marry a woman divorced from her husband; for the priest is holy to his God.' (Leviticus 21: 1, 4–7)

Besides discussing the ritual for the festivals of Passover, Weeks and Booths (see Chapter 2, Part 4), instructions are given for the great fast of the Day of Atonement:

> And the Lord said to Moses, 'On the tenth day of this seventh month is the day of atonement; it shall be for you a time of holy convocation, and you shall afflict yourselves and present an offering to God by fire to the Lord. And you shall do no work on this same day, for it is a day of atonement, to make atonement for you before the Lord your God . . . It shall be to you a

sabbath of solemn rest, and you shall afflict yourselves; on the ninth day of the month beginning at evening, from evening to evening shall you keep your sabbath.' (Leviticus 23: 26–8, 32)

The weekly Sabbath, the seventh day of rest, is emphasized in the P version of the Creation story:

Thus the heavens and the earth were finished, and all the host of them. And on the seventh day God finished his work which he had done, and he rested on the seventh day from all his work which he had done. So God blessed the seventh day and hallowed it, because on it God rested from all his work which he had done in Creation. (Genesis 2: 1–3)

The importance of the Sabbath is reiterated elsewhere in the Holiness Code:

The Lord said to Moses, 'Say to the people of Israel, six days shall work be done, but on the seventh day is a sabbath of solemn rest, a holy convocation; you shall do no work; it is a sabbath to the Lord in all your dwellings.' (Leviticus 24: 1, 3)

It is to the P writer that the Jewish people owe many of their food laws:

And the Lord said to Moses and Aaron, 'Say to the people of Israel, these are the living things which you may eat among all the beasts that are on the earth. Whatever parts the hoof and is cloven-footed and chews the cud, among the animals, you may eat . . . the swine because it parts the hoof and is cloven-footed, but does not chew the cud is unclean to you . . . These you may eat, of all that are in the waters. Everything in the waters that has fins and scales, whether in the seas or the rivers that has not fins and scales, of the swarming creatures in the waters and of the living creatures that are in the waters, is an abomination to you . . . And these you shall have in abomination among the birds, they shall not be eaten, they are an abomination: the eagle, the vulture, the osprey, the kite, the falcon according to its kind, every raven according to its kind, the ostrich, the nighthawk, the seagull, the hawk according to its kind.' (Leviticus 11: 1–3, 7, 9–10, 13–16)

For the life of every creature is the blood of it; therefore I have said to the people of Israel, you shall not eat the blood of any creature, for the life of every creature is its blood; whoever eats it shall be cut off. (Leviticus 17: 14)

The P writer has his own account of the covenant with Abraham and the institution of the rite of circumcision for all Jewish males:

And God said to Abraham, 'As for you, you shall keep my covenant, you and your descendants after you throughout their generations. This is my covenant, which you shall keep between me and you and your descendants after you; every male among you shall be circumcised. You shall be circumcised in the flesh of your foreskins, and it shall be a sign of the covenant between me and you. He that is eight days old among you shall be circumcised; every male throughout your generations.' (Genesis 17: 9–12)

Most scholars believe that the P source was compiled at the time of the Exile (see Chapter 4, Part 1) and the writer's understanding of the role of the Jewish people enabled the Israelites to survive the catastrophe of the destruction of the Temple in 586 BCE. Since then the rite of circumcision, the food laws and the keeping of the Sabbath and festivals have been crucial elements in the preservation of the Jews through the ages.

Chronological Table

Circa BCE	Documents	Events in Jewish History
2000–1800		
1800–1600		Age of the Patriarchs c. 1900–1600
1600–1400		
1400–1200	Whole Pentateuch – (Mosaic hypothesis)	Era of the Exodus c. 1400–1200
1000–800	J source (documentary hypothesis)	Era of the United and Divided Monarchies c. 1030–721
800–600	E source, D source (documentary hypothesis)	722 Northern Kingdom destroyed by Assyria
600–400	P source (documentary hypothesis)	586 Destruction of Southern Kingdom Babylonian Exile c. 586–538

Suggested Further Reading

The books of Leviticus, Numbers and Deuteronomy.

A. Cohen, ed., *The Soncino Chumash*, Brooklyn, NJ: Soncino Press, 1947.

R. Rendtorff, 'The Problem of the Process of Transmission in the Pentateuch', (trans. J. J. Scullion), *Journal for the Study of the Old Testament*, Supplement Series, 1990.

J. Wellhausen, *Prolegomena to the History of Israel*, Atlanta, GA: Scholars Press, 1994.

3

From Conquest to Exile

1. Conquest and Settlement

The biblical book of Joshua describes the Israelite settlement of the Promised Land as a conquest:

> After the death of Moses, the servant of the Lord, the Lord sent to Joshua the son of Nun, Moses' minister, 'Moses my servant is dead; now therefore arise, go over this Jordan, you and all this people, into the land which I am giving to them to the people of Israel. Every place that the sole of your foot will tread upon I have given to you, as I promised to Moses.' (Joshua 1: 1–3)

> Now Jericho was shut up from within and from without because of the people of Israel; none went out and none came in. And the Lord said to Joshua, 'See I have given into your hand Jericho, with its king and mighty men of valour . . .' So the people shouted and the trumpets were blown. As soon as the people heard the sound of the trumpet, the people raised a great shout, and the wall fell down flat, so that the people went up into the city, every man straight before him and they took the city. Then they destroyed all in the city, both men and women, young and old, oxen, sheep and asses, with the edge of the sword. (Joshua 6: 1–2, 20–1)

> And the Lord said to Joshua, 'Do not fear or be dismayed; take all the fighting men with you and arise, go up to Ai; see, I have given into your hand the King of Ai and his people, his city and his land.' . . . So Joshua burned the city of Ai and made it for ever a heap of ruins, as it is to this day. (Joshua 8: 1, 28)

There is, in fact, no archaeological evidence that either Ai or Jericho were destroyed at this period.

> So Joshua defeated the whole land, the hill country and the Negeb and the lowland and the slopes and all their kings; he left none remaining, but

utterly destroyed all that breathed, as the Lord God of Israel commanded.
(Joshua 10: 40)

This picture of the settlement has been disputed since the early years of
this century:

> Although there are many gaps in the sources and we must proceed with
> caution, the story of the Israelite settlement of Palestine can be summarized
> thus: the Israelites only occupied the parts of the country which were
> already large political units and which remained so afterwards, that is, the
> mountainous areas which had hardly been affected by the spread of the city-
> state. At the time these lands were not politically well organized; they prob-
> ably had a small population and were not yet capable of stemming the
> advance of the Israelites. They offered the Israelites their best chance of set-
> tling and exchanging their semi-nomadic way of life for one of farming.
> The city-states, by contrast, were established on the plains and had little con-
> tact with the Israelite infiltration except in their outlying areas; only a small
> part of the civic system was destroyed immediately. The city-state was only
> finally overcome when the Israelites adopted a policy of political expansion
> at the start of the first millennium. (Albrecht Alt, *Die Landnahme der Israeliten
> in Palästina*)

The book of Judges gives a different picture from the book of Joshua:

> And the people of Israel did what was evil in the sight of the Lord and also
> served the Baals; and they forsook the Lord, the God of their fathers who
> had brought them out of the land of Egypt . . . So the anger of the Lord
> was kindled against Israel, and he gave them over to plunderers who plun-
> dered them . . . Then the Lord raised up judges, who saved them out of the
> power of those who plundered them. (Judges 2: 11, 14, 16)

At this period the twelve tribes do not always seem to have co-operated
together as is illustrated by the ancient Song of Deborah:

> Awake awake Deborah! Awake awake, utter a song,
> Arise Barak, lead away your captives, O son of Abinoam.
> Then down marched the remnant of the noble; the people of the Lord
> marched down for him against the mighty.
> From Ephraim they set out thither into the valley, following you, Benjamin,
> with your kinsmen;
> From Machir marched down the commanders, and from Zebulun those who
> bear the marshal's staff;
> The princes of Issachar came with Deborah, and Issachar faithful to Barak;

into the valley they rushed forth at his heels.
Among the clans of Reuben there were great searchings of heart.
Why did you tarry among the sheepfolds, to hear the piping for the flocks?
Among the clans of Reuben there were great searchings of heart.
Gilead stayed beyond the Jordan; and Dan, why did he abide with the ships?
Asher sat still at the coast of the sea, settling down by his landings.
Zebulun is a people that jeoparded their lives to the death; Naphtali too on the heights of the field . . .
So perish all thine enemies O Lord. But thy friends be like the sun as he rises in his might. (Judges 5: 12–18, 31)

The German scholar Martin Noth, however, argued that the number twelve was of particular significance for the Israelites:

The Israelite twelve-tribe system is not an isolated phenomenon and cannot therefore be historically accounted for by the existence of twelve brothers as the tribes' ancestors or as a later artificially constructed model of the dividing up of a larger whole; in fact the number twelve is the result of definite established principles which were usual in tribal societies . . . There seem to have been practical reasons for the fixed number of twelve in that the members of these tribal associations had to take responsibility for the maintenance of and worship at the common shrine in a monthly rota. (Martin Noth, *Geschichte Israels*)

During the period of the Judges there seems to have been great resistance to the idea of having a king like other nations:

Then the men of Israel said to Gideon, 'Rule over us, you and your son and your grandson also; for you have delivered us out of the hand of Midian.' Gideon said to them, 'I will not rule over you, and my son will not rule over you; the Lord will rule over you.' (Judges 8: 22–3)

The first reference to Israel outside the Bible occurred in the time of the Judges:

Canaan is beset with every ill; Ashkelon is captured; Gezer has been taken; Yanoam no longer exists;
Israel lies desolate; its seed will not survive;
The land of the Hurrians is now a widow because of Egypt;
And all the lands everywhere are at peace.
All the nomads are now under the control of King Merenptah.
(Stela of Pharaoh Merenptah, 1223–1211 BCE)

2. The United Monarchy

Around 1050 BCE the pressure of outside enemies induced the Israelites to choose a king:

> The people refused to listen to the voice of Samuel; and they said, 'No! but we will have a king over us that we also may be like all the nations, and that our king may govern us and go out before us and fight our battles.' (I Samuel 8: 19–20)

Saul was anointed the first king of the twelve tribes, but at the end of his reign he committed suicide after being defeated by the Philistines; his death was lamented by his young successor David:

> Thy glory O Israel is slain upon thy high places! How are the mighty fallen!
> Tell it not in Gath, publish it not in the streets of Ashkelon;
> Lest the daughters of the Philistines rejoice, lest the daughters of the uncircumcised exult . . .
> Saul and Jonathan, beloved and lovely! In life and in death they were not divided;
> They were swifter than eagles, they were stronger than lions . . .
> How are the mighty fallen in the midst of the battle! . . .
> How are the mighty fallen and the weapons of war perished!
> (II Samuel 1: 19–20, 23, 25, 27)

It was David who captured the city of Jerusalem and made it his capital:

> And the king and his men went to Jerusalem against the Jebusites, the inhabitants of the land, who said to David, 'You will not come in here, but the blind and the lame will ward you off' – thinking, 'David cannot come in here.' Nevertheless David took the stronghold of Zion, that is the city of David . . . And David dwelt in the stronghold and called it the city of David . . . So David went and brought up the Ark of God from the house of Obed-edom to the City of David with rejoicing . . . And David danced before the Lord with all his might; and David was girded with a linen ephod. So David and all the house of Israel brought up the Ark of the Lord with shouting and with the sound of the horn. (II Samuel 5: 6–7, 9, 12b–15)

It is recorded that a new covenant was established between God and the house of David:

> I will sing of thy steadfast love, O Lord, for ever; with my mouth
> I will proclaim thy faithfulness to all generations.

For thy steadfast love was established for ever, thy faithfulness is firm as the heavens.
Thou hast said, 'I have made a covenant with my chosen one, I have sworn to David my servant;
'I will establish your descendants for ever, and build your throne for all generations.' (Psalms 89: 1–4)

and:

I have set my king on Zion, my holy hill. I will tell of the decree of the Lord; He said to me, 'You are my son, today I have begotten you.' (Psalms 2: 6–7)

At David's death, his son by his favourite wife Bathsheba succeeded him. It was Solomon who built the Temple in Jerusalem and established Israel as an international power in the ancient Near East:

Now when the Queen of Sheba heard of the fame of Solomon concerning the name of the Lord, she came to test him with hard questions. She came to Jerusalem with a very great retinue, with camels bearing spices, and very much gold and precious stones; and when she came to Solomon, she told him all that was on her mind. And Solomon answered all her questions; there was nothing hidden from the King which he could not explain to her. And when the Queen of Sheba had seen all the wisdom of Solomon, the house that he had built, the good of his table, the seating of his officials and the attendance of his servants, their clothing, his cupbearers and his burnt offerings which he offered at the house of the Lord, there was no more spirit in her. (I Kings 10: 1–5)

Among their legends, the Falashas, the black Jews of Ethiopia, claim to be descended from the Jews who accompanied Menelik, the supposed son of King Solomon and the Queen of Sheba, back to Ethiopia. The story continues that the Queen sent Menelik back to Jerusalem for his education and, when he returned home, he was accompanied by a group of Israelites who subsequently married native women.

For all his wealth and wisdom, however, King Solomon alienated his people. After his death, the Israelites petitioned his son Rehoboam:

'Your father made our yoke heavy. Now therefore lighten the hard service of your father and his heavy yoke upon us and we will serve you.' . . . And the King answered the people harshly, and forsaking the counsel which the old men had given him, he spoke to them according to the counsel of the young men saying, 'My father made your yoke heavy, but I will add to your yoke; my father chastised you with whips, but I will chastise you with scorpions.' (I Kings 12: 4, 13–14)

In consequence, in around 930 BCE, the ten northern tribes rebelled against the house of David and elected their own king, the young general Jeroboam. The two southern tribes, Judah and Benjamin, however, remained faithful.

3. The Divided Monarchy

In order to discourage pilgrimage to the south, King Jeroboam set up alternative shrines in the Northern Kingdom:

> And Jeroboam said in his heart, 'Now the kingdom will turn back to the house of David if this people go up to offer sacrifices in the house of the Lord at Jerusalem, then the heart of this people will turn again to their Lord, to Rehoboam King of Judah, and they will kill me and return to Rehoboam King of Judah.' So the King took counsel, and made two calves of gold. And he said to the people, 'You have gone up to Jerusalem long enough. Behold your gods, O Israel, who brought you up out of the land of Egypt.' And he set one in Bethel and the other he put in Dan. (I Kings 12: 26–9)

Since the writer of the books of Samuel and Kings was deeply influenced by the book of Deuteronomy (see Chapter 2, Part 4) all the northern kings in their turn were condemned for their rejection of the Jerusalem shrine:

> He did what was evil in the sight of the Lord, and walked in the way of Jeroboam and in his sin which he made Israel to sin. (I Kings 15: 34, etc.)

The biblical writers were more concerned with faithfulness to God than with political triumphs, but we know from the Moabite Stone that Omri, King of the Northern Kingdom (887–876 BCE) expanded his territory:

> Omri, King of Israel, oppressed Moab for many days, for Chemosh [the Moabite god] was angry with his land. And his son who succeeded him also said, 'I will oppress Moab.' (The Moabite Stone, Louvre Museum)

Omri's son, Ahab (876–853 BCE), who was married to the daughter of the powerful King of Phoenicia, was confronted by the mighty figure of the prophet Elijah:

> Now Elijah the Tishbite of Tishbe in Gilead said to Ahab, 'As the Lord the God of Israel lives, before whom I stand, there shall be neither dew nor rain

these years except by my word . . .' When Ahab saw Elijah Ahab said to him, 'Is it you, you troubler of Israel?' And he answered, 'I have not troubled Israel, but you have, and your father's house, because you have forsaken the commandments of the Lord and followed the Baals. Now therefore send and gather all Israel to meet at Mount Carmel . . .' So Ahab sent to all the people of Israel and gathered the prophets together at Mount Carmel. And Elijah came near to all the people and said, 'How long will you go limping with two different opinions? If the Lord is God, follow him, but if Baal, then follow him.' And the people did not answer him a word. (I Kings 17: 1; 18: 17–18, 20–1)

Later Elijah confronted the king over the theft of Naboth's vineyard:

Then the word of the Lord came to Elijah the Tishbite saying, 'Arise, go down to meet Ahab, King of Israel, who is in Samaria; behold he is in the vineyard of Naboth, where he has gone to take possession. And you shall say to him, "Thus says the Lord, 'Have you killed and also taken possession?'"' And you shall say to him, "Thus says the Lord, 'In the place where dogs licked up the blood of Naboth shall dogs lick your own blood.'"' Ahab said to Elijah, 'Have you found me, O my enemy?' He answered, 'I have found you because you have sold yourself to do what is evil in the sight of the Lord. Behold I will bring evil upon you; I will utterly sweep you away, and will cut off from Ahab every male, bond or free in Israel.' (I Kings 21: 17–21)

So towering was Elijah's reputation that after he left the earth in a fiery chariot, it was believed that he would return again before the final Day of the Lord:

Behold I will send you Elijah the prophet before the great and terrible day of the Lord comes. And he will turn the hearts of fathers to their children and the hearts of children to their fathers, lest I come and smite the land with a curse. (Malachi 4: 5–6)

Later, in the eighth century, people of both the Northern and Southern Kingdoms were reproved by a series of prophets for their idolatry and selfishness:

Therefore because you trample upon the poor and take from him exactions of wheat, you have built houses of hewn stone, but you shall not dwell in them; you have planted vineyards, but you shall not drink their wine. For I know how many are your transgressions, and how great are your sins – you who afflict the righteous, who take a bribe, and turn aside the needy in the gate. (Amos 5: 11–12)

Let justice roll down like waters and righteousness like an everflowing stream. (Amos 5: 24)

When Israel was a child I loved him, and out of Egypt I called my son. The more I called them, the more they went from me; they kept sacrificing to the Baals, and burning incense to idols. Yet it was I who taught Ephraim to walk, I took them up in my arms; but they did not know that I healed them. I led them with cords of compassion, with the bands of love, and I became to them as one who eases the yoke on their jaws and I bent down to them and fed them. They shall return to the land of Egypt, and Assyria shall be their king because they have refused to return to me. (Hosea 11: 1–5)

Will the Lord be pleased with thousands of rams and with ten thousand rivers of oil? Shall I give my first-born for my transgression, the fruit of my body for the sin of my soul? He has shown you, O man, what is good; and what does the Lord require of you but to do justice, and to love kindness and to walk humbly with your god. (Micah 6: 7–8)

Meanwhile, to the north-east, the Assyrian empire was expanding. The black obelisk of Shalmaneser III shows King Jehu of the Northern Kingdom (842–815 BCE) offering tribute to the Assyrian king. The inscription reads:

The tribute of Jehu, son of Omri. Silver, gold, a golden bowl, a golden vase, golden cups, golden buckets, tin, a staff for the royal hand, fruits. (The Black Obelisk, British Museum)

4. The End of the Northern Kingdom

In 724 BCE, the Assyrian king attacked the Northern Kingdom and the city of Samaria fell after a long siege:

In the twelfth year of Ahaz, King of Judah, Hoshea the son of Elah began to reign in Samaria over Israel and he reigned nine years. And he did what was evil in the sight of the Lord, yet not as the kings of Israel who were before him. Against him came up Shalmaneser, King of Assyria; and Hoshea became his vassal and paid him tribute. But the king of Assyria found treachery in Hoshea; for he had sent messages to So, King of Egypt, and offered no tribute to the king of Assyria, as he had done year by year; therefore the king of Assyria shut him up and bound him in prison. Then the king of Assyria invaded all the land and came to Samaria, and for three years he besieged it. In the ninth year of Hoshea the king of Assyria captured Samaria and he carried the Israelites away to Assyria and placed them in Halah and on the Habor, the river of Gozan, and in the cities of the Medes. (II Kings 17: 1–6)

According to the Assyrian records of the time:

I surrounded [the city of Samaria] and deported 27,290 of its inhabitants as prisoners as well as their chariots . . . and also the gods in whom they put their trust. I used them to equip 200 chariots for units in my army and the rest were made to live their lives within Assyria. I then restored the city of Samaria and made it more inhabitable than it was before. I brought into it conquered peoples from the countries which I myself had defeated. I set over them my official as governor of the district and counted them as people of Assyria itself. (Nimrud Prism, British Museum)

The Deuteronomic historian describes the new inhabitants of the Northern Kingdom:

And the King of Assyria brought people from Babylon, Cuthah, Avvah, Hamath and Sepharvaim, and placed them in the cities of Samaria instead of the people of Israel; and they took possession of Samaria and dwelt in its cities . . . One of the priests whom they had carried away from Samaria came and dwelt in Bethel, and he taught them how they should fear the Lord. But every nation still made gods of its own, and put them in the shrines of the high places which the Samaritans had made, every nation in the cities in which they dwelt . . . So they feared the Lord, but also served their own gods, after the manner of the nations from among whom they had been carried away. (II Kings 17: 24, 28, 29, 33)

What then happened to the Ten Lost Tribes, who, after all, were heirs to the promise to Abraham (see Chapter 1, Part 5)? Various speculations have been offered:

One part of Israel was exiled beyond the River Sambatyon, one part to Daphne near Antioch and the third part was covered by a cloud. (Jerusalem Talmud, Sanhedrin 10: 29c)

The River Sambatyon is full of sand and stones and on the six working days of the week, they tumble over each other with such vehemence that the crash and roar are heard far and wide. But on the Sabbath the tumultuous river subsides into quiet. As a guard against trespassers on that day, a cloud stretches along the whole length of the river, and none can approach Sambatyon within three miles. (L. Ginzberg, Legends of the Jews)

The Ten Tribes are beyond the Euphrates till now and are in immense multitude and not to be estimated in numbers. (Josephus, *Antiquities of the Jews*
11: 133)

Edward Hine sought to identify the lost tribes with the British nation in
his book *Forty-Seven Identifications of the British Nation with the Ten Lost
Tribes of Israel Founded upon Five Hundred Scriptural Proofs* published in 1871.

Nonetheless for centuries the hope was retained that the Ten Lost Tribes
would return in fulfilment of the promise:

Thus says the Lord God: Behold I will take the people of Israel from the
nations among which they have gone, and will gather them from all sides
and bring them to their own land, and I will make them one nation in the
land, upon the mountains of Israel; and one king shall be king over them
all; and they shall no longer be two nations and no longer divided into two
kingdoms. They shall not defile themselves any more with their idols and
their detestable things, or with any of their transgressions; but I will save them
from all the backslidings in which they have sinned, and will cleanse them;
and they shall be my people and I will be their God. (Ezekiel 37: 21–3)

Meanwhile Ahaz, King of the Southern Kingdom, continued to pay tribute to the Assyrian king and maintained a highly precarious independence:

So Ahaz sent messages to Tiglath-pileser, King of Assyria, saying, 'I am your
servant and your son . . .' Ahaz also took silver and gold that was found in
the house of the Lord and in the treasures of the King's house and sent a
present to the King of Assyria . . . When King Ahaz went to Damascus to
meet Tiglath-pileser, King of Assyria, he saw the altar that was in Damascus.
And King Ahaz sent to Uriah the priest a model of the altar, and its pattern,
exact in all its details. And Uriah the priest built the altar . . . And the covered way for the Sabbath which had been built inside the palace, and the
outer entrance for the King he removed from the house of the Lord, because
of the King of Assyria. (II Kings 16: 7a, 8, 10, 11a, 18)

5. The Babylonian Conquest

King Hezekiah of Judah (715–687 BCE) removed the Assyrian parapher-
nalia from the Temple and rebelled against the Assyrian King. After King
Sennacherib had marched against him, however, the tribute was resumed:

As for the Jew Hezekiah who did not bow down under my yoke, I besieged
and captured forty-six of his strong walled cities as well as the numberless

small cities in their neighbourhood . . . I took away 200, 150 people, great and small, male and female, horses, mules, donkeys, camels, cattle and sheep without number. I counted them as spoil. The King himself I shut up in Jerusalem, his royal city, like a bird in a cage . . . the awesome splendour of my majesty overcame him . . . He sent his messengers to pay tribute and to accept servitude. (Taylor Prism, British Museum)

Only when the power of Assyria began to wane did Hezekiah's great grandson Josiah (640–609 BCE) assert his independence by purging the Jerusalem Temple of all Assyrian influence. It was during his reign that the book of Deuteronomy (or something like it) was found (see Chapter 2, Part 4);

Then the King sent, and all the elders of Judah and Jerusalem were gathered to him. And the King went up to the house of the Lord, and with him all the men of Judah and all the inhabitants of Jerusalem, and the priests and the prophets, all the people both great and small; and he read in their hearing all the words of the book of the covenant which had been found in the house of the Lord. And the King stood by the pillar and made a covenant before the Lord, to walk after the Lord and to keep his commandments and his testimonies and his statutes, with all his heart and all his soul, to perform the words of this covenant that were written in this book; and all the people joined in the covenant. (II Kings 23: 1–3)

By the end of the seventh century BCE, Babylon had become the dominant power in the ancient Near East. The prophet Jeremiah warned the people of the fate that awaited them:

Thus said the Lord: Go, buy a potter's earthen flask, and take some of the elders of the people and some of the senior priests, and go out to the valley of the son of Hinnom at the entry of the Potsherd gate, and proclaim there the words that I tell you. You shall say: Hear the words of the Lord, O kings of Judah and inhabitants of Jerusalem. Thus says the Lord of Hosts, the God of Israel: Behold I am bringing such evil upon this place that the ears of every one who hears of it will tingle . . . Then you shall break the flask in the sight of the men who go with you, and shall say to them: Thus says the Lord of Hosts: So will I break this people and this city, as one breaks a potter's vessel, so that it can never be mended. (Jeremiah 19: 1–3, 10–11a)

The prophecy came true all too swiftly:

At that time the servants of Nebuchadnezzar, King of Babylon, came to the city while his servants were besieging it; and Jehoiachin King of Judah gave himself up to the King of Babylon, himself, and his mother, and his servants, and his princes, and his palace officials. The King of Babylon took him prisoner in the eighth year of his reign. (II Kings 24: 10–12)

King Zedekiah (597–589 BCE), who succeeded Jehoiachin, was not content to be a vassal of Babylon:

And Zedekiah rebelled against the King of Babylon. And in the ninth year of his reign, in the tenth month, on the tenth day of the month, Nebuchadnezzar, King of Babylon, came with all his army against Jerusalem, and laid siege to it; and they built siegeworks against it round about. So the city was besieged till the eleventh year of King Zedekiah. On the ninth day of the fourth month the famine was so severe in the city that there was no food for the people of the land. Then a breach was made in the city; the King with all the men of war fled by night by way of the gate between the two walls, by the King's garden, though the Chaldeans were around the city. And they went in the direction of Arabah. But the army of the Chaldeans pursued the King and overtook him in the plains of Jericho; and all his army was scattered from him. Then they captured the King, and brought him up to the King of Babylon at Riblah, who passed sentence upon him. They slew the sons of Zedekiah before his eyes, and put out the eyes of Zedekiah, and bound him in fetters and took him to Babylon. In the fifth month, on the seventh day of the month – which was the nineteenth year of King Nebuchadnezzar, King of Babylon – Nebuzaradan, the captain of the bodyguard, a servant of the King of Babylon, came to Jerusalem. And he burned the house of the Lord, and the King's house and all the houses of Jerusalem: every great house he burned down. (II Kings 25: 1–9)

The desperate situation is reflected in potsherds found in the garrison town of Lachish near Jerusalem:

We are looking for the lights of Lachish, according to the signs which my Lord has given, for we cannot see Azekah. (Lachish Letters, British Museum)

The people of the Southern Kingdom were taken into exile and the desolation of the plundered city of Jerusalem is described in the book of Lamentations:

How lonely sits the city that was full of people!
How like a widow has she become, she that was great among the nations!
She that was a princess among the cities has become a vassal . . .
Judah has gone into exile because of affliction and hard servitude.

She dwells now among the nations, and finds no resting place.
Her pursuers have all overtaken her in the midst of her distress.

(Lamentations 1: 1, 3)

Chronological Table

Circa BCE	Documents	Events in Jewish History
1300–1200	Stele of Merenptah	
1200–1100	? Song of Deborah	Era of the Judges
1100–1000		c. 1030 Beginning of United Monarchy
1000–900	? Liturgical Psalms	c. 930 Beginning of Divided Monarchy
900–800	Moabite Stone; Black Obelisk	
800–700	Amos; Hosea; Nimrud Prism	722 Northern Kingdom destroyed by Assyria
700–600	Micah; Deuteronomy; Taylor Prism	
600–500	Jeremiah; Ezekiel; Lamentations; Joshua; Judges; I and II Samuel; I and II Kings; Lachish Letters	786 Destruction of Jerusalem Babylonian Exile c. 586–538

Suggested Further Reading

The books of Joshua, Judges, I and II Samuel, I and II Kings.

I. Finkelstein, *The Archaeology of the Israelite Settlement*, Jerusalem: Israel Exploration Society, 1988.

M. Noth, 'The Deuteronomic History', *Journal for the Society of the Old Testament Press*, 1981.

J. F. A. Sawyer, *Prophecy and the Prophets of the Old Testament*, Oxford: Oxford University Press, 1987.

4

From Restoration to Destruction

1. Exile

The loss of the Temple in Jerusalem and exile in a foreign land were devastating experiences:

> By the waters of Babylon, there we sat and wept when we remembered
> Zion,
> On the willows there we hung up our lyres
> For there our captors required of us songs, and our tormentors mirth, saying
> 'Sing us one of the songs of Zion!'
> How shall we sing the Lord's song in a strange land?
> If I forget you, O Jerusalem, let my right hand wither!
> Let my tongue cleave to the roof of my mouth if I do not remember
> you,
> If I do not set Jerusalem above my highest joy! (Psalms 137: 1–6)

In fact there is evidence that many of the Jewish exiles prospered in Babylon:

> Then the King commanded Ashpenaz, his chief eunuch, to bring some
> of the people of Israel, both of the royal family and of the nobility, youth
> without blemish, handsome and skilful in all wisdom, endowed with
> understanding, learning, and competent to serve in the King's palace, and
> to teach them the letters and language of the Chaldeans. The King
> assigned them a daily portion of the rich food which the King ate, and
> of the wine which he drank. They were to be educated for three years
> and at the end of that time they were to stand before the King. (Daniel
> 1: 3–5)

> Then the King gave Daniel high honours and many great gifts, and made
> him ruler over the whole province of Babylon and chief prefect over all the
> wise men of Babylon. (Daniel 2: 48)

Then the King promoted Shadrach, Meshach and Abednego in the province of Babylon. (Daniel, 3: 30)

It is generally thought that the synagogue, as a community institution, began during the period of the Babylonian exile:

Thus says the Lord God. Though I removed them far off among the nations, and though I scattered them among the countries, yet I have been a sanctuary to them for a while in the countries where they have gone. (Ezekiel 11: 16)

The Deuteronomic histories (Joshua, Judges, I and II Samuel and I and II Kings) were probably compiled at this time and they explain the calamity in the light of Israel's unfaithfulness to God. Nonetheless, the books end on a note of hope:

And in the thirty-seventh year of the exile of Jehoiachin, King of Judah, in the twelfth month on the twenty-seventh day of the month, Evil-Merodach, King of Babylon, in the year that he began to reign, graciously freed Jehoiachin, King of Judah, from prison; and he spoke kindly to him and gave him a seat above the seats of the kings who were with him in Babylon. So Jehoiachin put off his prison garments. And every day of his life he dined regularly at the King's table; and for his allowance, a regular allowance was given him by the King, every day a portion, as long as he lived. (II Kings 25: 27–30)

In the event the Babylonians were not invincible:

Thus says the Lord, your Redeemer, the Holy One of Israel: for your sake I will send to Babylon and break down all the bars, and the shouting of the Chaldeans will be turned to lamentations. I am the Lord, your Holy One, the Creator of Israel, your King. (Isaiah 43: 14–15)

The prophet predicted that Cyrus, King of Persia, would be the agent of Babylon's destruction:

Thus says the Lord, your Redeemer, who formed you from the womb. I am the Lord who made all things, who stretched out the heavens alone, who spread out the earth – who was with me? . . . who says of Cyrus, 'He is my shepherd, and he shall fulfil my purpose,' saying of Jerusalem, 'She shall be built,' and of the temple, 'Your foundation shall be laid.' Thus says the Lord to his anointed, to Cyrus, whose right hand I have grasped, to subdue nations before him and ungird the loins of kings, to open doors before him that gates may not be closed. (Isaiah 44: 24, 28; 45: 1)

In 539 BCE, Babylon was conquered by Cyrus:

> In the month of Teshrit, Cyrus was waging war on the Babylonian army at Opis by the River Tigris. The people of Babylon panicked and rose in revolt, but [King Nabonidus] killed the people. Then on the fifteenth day, Sipper was taken without a fight and Nabonidus fled. On the sixteenth day, the local governor of Gutium, Ugbaru, together with the troops of Cyrus entered [the city of] Babylon without a battle. Later Nabonidus was taken prisoner after he came back to Babylon . . . On the third day of Marcheswan, Cyrus entered Babylon and branches were waved before him. Peace was restored to the city. Cyrus proclaimed peace to Babylon. (Nabonidus Chronicle)

The triumph of Cyrus is also recorded in the Cyrus Cylinder:

> [The god] Marduk, the mighty Lord, compassionate to his own people, looked with happiness on [Cyrus'] good deeds and his righteous intentions. He ordered him to go against the city of Babylon. He guided him on the road to Babylon and walked by his side like a friend and comrade. His huge army, which was numberless like the waters of a river, stayed close with their armour, and moved on beside him. He let him into his city of Babylon without a battle or a skirmish. He averted any hardship from Babylon. He ended the rule of Nabonidus, the king who showed him no reverence. All the people of Babylon, all of Sumer and Akkad, princes and governors, bowed before him [Cyrus] and kissed his feet. They were delighted he was king. Their faces beamed. (Cyrus Cylinder, British Museum)

2. Return and Renewal

The Persian record also indicates that exiled people were allowed to return to their homelands:

> To the cities of Ashur and Susa, Agade, Eshunna, the cities of Zamban, Meturnu, Der, as far as the region of the land of Gutium, the holy cities beyond the Tigris. Their sanctuaries had been in ruins for many years; I returned the gods who had been in the midst of them, I put them back in their places and gave them lasting dwelling places. I assembled all the inhabitants and gave them back their dwelling places. (Cyrus Cylinder, British Museum)

According to the biblical record, the Jews were allowed to return to the Promised Land:

In the first year of Cyrus, King of Persia, that the word of the Lord by the mouth of Jeremiah might be accomplished, the Lord stirred up the spirit of Cyrus, King of Persia so that he made a proclamation throughout all his kingdom and also put it writing: 'Thus says Cyrus, King of Persia. The Lord, the God of Heaven, has given me all the kingdoms of the earth, and he has charged me to build him a house at Jerusalem, which is in Judah. Whoever is among you of all his people, may his God be with him, and let him go up to Jerusalem, which is in Judah, and rebuild the house of the Lord, the God of Israel – he is the God who is in Jerusalem.' (Ezra 1: 1–3)

The rebuilding party was led by Zerubbabel, a grandson of Jehoiachin, who was supported by the priest Joshua. The messianic hope – the belief that another Davidic king would emerge who would establish God's kingdom on earth – dates from this era:

Speak to Zerubbabel, governor of Judah, saying, I am about to shake the heavens and the earth, and to overthrow the thrones of kingdoms; I am about to destroy the strength of the kingdoms of the nations, and overthrow the chariots and their riders; and the horses and their riders shall go down, every one by the sword of his fellow. On that day, says the Lord of Hosts, I will take you, O Zerubbabel, my servant, the son of Shealtiel, says the Lord, and make you like a signet ring; for I have chosen you, says the Lord of Hosts. (Haggai 2: 20–3)

The Samaritans, descendants of the inhabitants of the Northern Kingdom (see Chapter 3, Part 4) were not permitted to help with the rebuilding:

They approached Zerubbabel and the heads of fathers' houses and said to them, 'Let us build with you; for we worship your God as you do, and we have been sacrificing to him since the days of Esar-haddon, King of Assyria, who brought us here.' But Zerubbabel, Jeshua, and the rest of the heads of fathers' houses in Israel said to them, 'You have nothing to do with us in building a house to our God; but we alone will build to the Lord, the God of Israel.' (Ezra 4: 2–3)

In consequence there was enmity between the Samaritans and the Jews, and the Samaritans developed their own traditions centred on Mount Gerizim:

When the Lord your God brings you into the land of Canaan which you are entering to take possession of, you shall set up there stones and plaster them with plaster, and you shall write upon them all the words of the Law. And when you have gone over Jordan, you shall set up these stones, concerning which I command you this day, on Mount Gerizim. And you shall build an altar to the Lord your God. (Samaritan Pentateuch)

Things do not seem to have gone smoothly for the returning exiles. Many seem to have fallen away:

Then I will draw near to you for judgement; I will be a swift witness against the sorceress, against the adulteress, against those who swear falsely, against those who oppress the hireling in his wages, the widow and the orphan, against those who thrust aside the sojourner, and do not fear me, says the Lord of Hosts. (Malachi 3: 5)

The situation was transformed by Nehemiah, who was appointed governor of Judah in 445 BCE and the scribe Ezra, who read the Law to the people, helped them to observe the festivals and who insisted that they divorce their foreign wives:

And Ezra the priest brought the law before the assembly, both men and women, and all who could hear with understanding, on the first day of the seventh month. And he read from it facing the square before the Water Gate from early morning until midday, in the presence of the men and the women and those who could understand; and the ears of all the people were attentive to the book of the Law. (Nehemiah 8: 2–3)

And Nehemiah who was the governor, and Ezra the priest and scribe, and the Levites who taught the people said to all the people, 'This day is holy to the Lord your God; do not mourn or weep.' For all the people wept when they heard the words of the Law. (Nehemiah 8: 9)

In those days also I saw the Jews who had married women of Ashdod, Ammon and Moab . . . and I contended with them and I cursed them and beat some of them and pulled out their hair; and I made them take oath in the name of God, saying, 'You shall not give your daughters to their sons, or take their daughters for your sons or for yourselves.' (Nehemiah 13: 23–5)

Not everyone accepted Ezra and Nehemiah's policy of racial purity as is shown in the book of Ruth written about this time. It is the story of a Moabite woman who became the great grandmother of King David:

So Boaz took Ruth and she became his wife; and he went in to her, and the Lord gave her conception and she bore a son . . . They named him Obed; he was father of Jesse, the father of David. (Ruth 4: 13, 17b)

In 333 BCE, King Darius of Persia was defeated by the young King Alexander of Macedonia and Judah became part of the Macedonian empire ruled initially by King Ptolemy of Egypt from Alexandria. At this time colonies of Jews were springing up all round the Mediterranean Sea and it became necessary to translate the scriptures into Greek. The translation was known as the Septuagint. The first-century historian Josephus gives us an account of its origin:

> [The seventy-two translators] began working as carefully and ambitiously as possible in order to make the translation accurate . . . Each day they used to attend court to pay their respects to Ptolemy and then they returned to that place. They washed their hands in the sea and purified themselves and then, fully cleansed, they worked on translating the Law. When the Law had been transcribed and the translation was finished at the end of seventy-five days, Demetrius gathered together all the Jews and read the laws aloud in front of the translators. Then the people expressed their approval. (Josephus, *Antiquities of the Jews* XII)

3. The Maccabean Revolt and its Aftermath

By 198 BCE, King Antiochus III of the Selucid dynasty had taken over the territory of Judah (or Judea as it was called in Greek) from the Ptolemaic kings:

> And the King of the north [Antiochus] shall come and throw up siege-works and take a well-fortified city. And the forces of the south [the Ptolemies] shall not stand, or even his picked troops, for there shall be no strength to stand. (Daniel 11: 15)

With the accession of Antiochus IV (Epiphanes) (175–163 BCE), an attempt was made by the authorities to Hellenize Jerusalem and outlaw the Jewish religion:

> The King set up a pagan altar in place of the altar in the Temple and he slaughtered pigs on it – which was a type of sacrifice which was neither lawful nor customary in the worship of the Jews. He forced them to give up worshipping their own God and instead bow down to the gods in whom he believed; he then ordered them to build shrines in every town and vil-

lage and to put up altars on which to sacrifice pigs every day. He also gave orders that they were not to circumcise their children. (Josephus, *Antiquities of the Jews* XII)

Harsh and utterly grievous was the onslaught of evil. For the Temple was filled with debauchery and revelling by the Gentiles, who dallied with harlots and had intercourse with women within the sacred precincts, and besides brought in things for sacrifice that were unfit. The altar was covered with abominable offerings which were forbidden by the laws. A man could neither keep the Sabbath, nor observe the feasts of his fathers, nor so much as confess himself to be a Jew. (II Maccabees 6: 3–6)

Led by the Hasmonean family (the Maccabees), the Jews rose in revolt and in 164 BCE succeeded in recapturing Jerusalem and rededicating the Temple:

They celebrated the dedication of the altar for eight days and offered burnt offerings with gladness; they offered a sacrifice of deliverance and praise . . . There was very great gladness among the people and the reproach of the Gentiles was removed. Then Judas and his brothers and all the assembly of Israel determined that every year at that season the days of dedication of the altars should be observed with gladness and joy for eight days. (I Maccabees 4: 56, 58–9)

The Hasmonean family succeeded in founding a dynasty of both rulers and high priests; they extended the territory of Judea and, for a short period, there was a precariously independent Jewish state:

He established peace in the land, and Israel rejoiced with great joy,
Each man sat under his vine and his fig tree, and there was none to make them afraid,
No one was left in the land to fight them, and the kings were crushed in those days. (I Maccabees 14: 11–13)

However, by the middle of the first century BCE, the Roman general Pompey had turned Judea into a client state of the Roman empire. Herod of Idumea with a Roman army laid siege to Jerusalem and conquered Judea in 37 BCE and was designated King by his Roman allies:

[Mark] Antony came forward and told the Senate that in the war against the Parthians it was to their advantage that Herod should become King. Everyone thought this a good idea, so they voted for the proposal. (Josephus, *Antiquities of the Jews* XXII)

Throughout his long reign Herod (37–4 BCE) was hated as a traitor and a tyrant. Nonetheless, he made an attempt to win popularity and one of his projects was a magnificent rebuilding of the Temple in Jerusalem:

> Then in the eighteenth year of his reign . . . Herod undertook the astonishing task of rebuilding, at his own expense, the Temple of God by enlarging its precincts and building it up to a more impressive height. He believed that fulfilling this task would be his most noteworthy achievement (as indeed proved to be the case) and would by itself be significant enough to ensure that he would be remembered for ever . . . The King never entered any of the inner courts because he was not a priest and so was prevented. But he concerned himself with the construction of the porticos and the outer courts and these buildings were finished in eight years. The inner sanctuary was built by the priests in one year and six months and all the people rejoiced and gave thanks to God . . . It just happened that the day on which the building work was finished was the same as the anniversary of the King's accession which they were accustomed to observe. Because of the double celebration, the festival was extremely splendid. (Ibid., XV)

Josephus' epitaph for the King is worth noting:

> He was a man who was cruel to everyone; he yielded to anger easily and despised justice. Nonetheless, he was as favoured by fortune as anyone has ever been, since he became King from being a commoner. Although he was surrounded by innumerable dangers, he managed to evade them all and he survived to a very great age. He himself believed that in his household affairs and in his relations with his sons he had been very lucky since he invariably got the better of those he considered to be his enemies. But I personally think he was very unfortunate indeed. (Ibid., XVII)

4. Pharisees, Sadducees and Essenes

During the Hasmonean period various sects appeared among the Jews of Judea, who are familiar from the New Testament:

> Then said Jesus to the crowds and to his disciples, 'The Scribes and the Pharisees sit on Moses' seat; so practise and observe whatever they tell you, but not what they do; for they preach but do not practise. They bind hard burdens, hard to bear, and lay them on men's shoulders; but they themselves will not move them with their finger. They do all their deeds to be seen by men; for they make their phylacteries broad and their fringes long and they love the place of honour at feasts and the best seats in the synagogue and salutations in the market place, and being called rabbi by men.' (Matthew 23: 1–7)

The same day Sadducees came to him, who say there is no resurrection. (Matthew 22: 23)

In general the New Testament gives a very negative picture of Jews and Judaism. More sympathetic portraits emerge in the works of Josephus, in the Mishnah (see Chapter 5, Part 2) and in the Dead Sea Scrolls:

The Pharisees [were] a Jewish sect who seemed to be more pious than everyone else and more particular in their interpretation of the law. (Josephus, *The Jewish War* I)

The Pharisees are considered to be the most expert interpreters of the Law and are held to be the leading sect. They account for everything either by fate or by God; the choice between doing right or wrong rests mainly with human beings, but in every action fate plays some part. Every soul is incorruptible, but only the souls of the virtuous pass into other bodies; the souls of the wicked are eternally punished. (Ibid., II)

The Pharisees live very simply, making no concession to luxury. They follow their own particular doctrines which have been selected and transmitted as being virtuous, and they attach the most importance to the keeping of those commandments which have been laid down for them in the tradition. They show respect and reverence for their elders and they do not presume to question their precepts lightly. (Josephus, *Antiquities of the Jews* VIII)

Hillel [a leading Pharisee] said: Be of the disciples of Aaron who love peace and pursue it; so you should love all men and attract them to the study of the Law. He used to say: Whoever magnifies his own name destroys it; whoever does not increase his knowledge of the Law shall be cut off; whoever does not study the Law deserves death; and whoever gives himself the crown of the Law shall be consumed. He also said: If I do not do good works, then who will do them for me? And if I think only of myself, then what am I? And if not now, when? Shammai [another Pharisee leader] used to say: Let your study of the Law be fixed; say little and do much and receive all men with cheerfulness. (Mishnah, Avoth I)

We only see the Sadducees through the eyes of their opponents since they left no records of their own. They were a small group of hereditary priests who controlled the worship in the Temple:

The Sadducees do not believe in the existence of fate and they maintain that God can neither commit sin nor see it. They insist that men are free to choose between good and evil and every person must decide for himself.

They completely deny the permanence of the soul, punishment in Hades and future rewards. Again the Pharisees are friendly to each other and try to promote peace among the public at large, but the Sadducees show a more disagreeable spirit even among themselves. (Josephus, *The Jewish War* II)

The daughters of the Sadducees, if they follow after the customs of their fathers, must be considered to be like the women of the Samaritans [see Chapter 4, Part 2]; but if they have separated themselves and follow after the customs of the Israelites, they must be considered to be like the women of the Israelites. (Mishnah, Niddah IV)

When Paul [the Christian apostle] perceived that one part [of the Council] were Sadducees and the other Pharisees, he cried out in the council, 'Brethren, I am a Pharisee, the son of a Pharisee; with respect to the hope and the resurrection of the dead I am on trial.' And when he had said this, a dissension arose between the Pharisees and the Sadducees; and the assembly was divided. For the Sadducees say there is no resurrection, nor angel, nor spirit; but the Pharisees acknowledge them all. (Acts 23: 6–8)

The Essenes seem to have been a monastic group. The sect who lived at Qumran and who produced the Dead Sea Scrolls shared many of the characteristics of the Essenes as described by Josephus:

They do not have a single city, but there are large colonies of them everywhere . . . When they travel, they carry no luggage at all . . . In clothing and personal appearance, they are like children in the care of a strict tutor. They do not change their clothes or their shoes until they are dropping to pieces or worn out with age . . . They show their devotion to God in a unique way. Before dawn they say nothing about ordinary matters, but they offer up traditional prayers as if they were begging God to appear. Then they are sent by their supervisors to work, each man to the occupation that he understands best, and they work very hard until an hour before midday. Then they meet again together in one place, put on linen loin cloths and wash all over in cold water. Once purified, they go into a building which no one outside their community may enter . . . After breakfast . . . they go back to work until the evening . . . Neither shouting nor disorder ever desecrates their house . . . It is their unshakeable belief that while their bodies are corruptible and their flesh impermanent, their souls are immortal for ever. They come down from the most rarefied ether and they are trapped in the prison of the body . . . but once freed from the bonds of the flesh, like a man released from years of slavery, they rejoice and soar above. (Josephus, *The Jewish War* II)

Whoever comes before the council of the community is entering into a covenant with God before all those who have also freely promised themselves. He will swear a binding oath that he will return with his whole heart and soul to every commandment of Moses' law in accordance with the revelations of the sons of Zadok, the keepers of the covenant and the seekers of his will, and to the crowd of the men of the covenant who have all together dedicated themselves to his truth and to walking in the path of his joy. And by the covenant, he will promise to separate himself from all the men of lies who continue to walk in the path of wickedness. (Dead Sea Scrolls, Manual of Discipline V)

5. The Jewish War

In the first century CE there was continual discontent among the Jews of Judea. Jesus of Nazareth was the leader of one of several messianic movements of the period:

But a Pharisee in the Council named Gamaliel, a teacher of the law, held in honour by all the people, stood up and ordered the men [followers of Jesus] to be put outside for a while. And he said to them, 'Men of Israel, take care what you do with these men. For before these days Theudas arose, giving himself out to be somebody, and a number of men, about four hundred, joined him, but he was slain and all who followed him were dispersed and came to nothing. After him Judas the Galilean arose in the days of the census and drew away some of the people after him; he also perished, and all who followed him were scattered. So in the present case, I tell you, keep away from these men and let them alone; for if this plan or this undertaking is of men it will fail; but if it is of God, you will not be able to overthrow them. You might even be found opposing God.' (Acts 5: 34–9)

Pontius Pilate, the Roman Procurator mentioned in the Gospels, was particularly insensitive to the Jews:

Tiberius sent Pilate as Procurator of Judea. During the night he secretly and under cover sent images of Caesar to Jerusalem. At dawn they caused enormous consternation among the Jews. Those who were nearby were amazed when they saw the images because it meant that their laws had been defied (Jews do not allow any graven images to be set up in the city). The furious city crowd were joined by a huge multitude of people from the country. They hurried to Caesarea to see Pilate and they entreated him to remove the images from Jerusalem and to respect their traditional laws. When Pilate refused their request, they fell on their faces all around his house and lay without moving for five days and five nights . . .

Later Pilate stirred up more trouble by using the sacred treasure of the Temple for building a five mile aqueduct. (Josephus, *The Jewish War* II)

Among the Jews various nationalist groups arose to oppose the Romans:

> When the bandits had been cleared from the countryside, another group
> sprang up in Jerusalem known as the Daggermen. They committed many
> murders in broad daylight in the middle of the city. One of their favourite
> exploits was to mingle with the crowds on festival days. They would con-
> ceal in their clothes a small dagger which they used to stab their opponents.
> When the chosen victim fell, the murderers melted away in the angry crowd
> and, because they were so plausible, they were not detected. The first to have
> his throat cut by them was Jonathan, the High Priest . . .
>
> Another group of criminals did an equal amount of damage as the mur-
> derers to the smooth running of Jerusalem. They were cheats and deceivers,
> but they claimed to be inspired. They plotted to bring about change and
> revolution by inciting the crowds to behave as if they were possessed. They
> led the people out into the wild country, persuading them that God would
> give them a sign of the coming freedom. (Ibid.)

The rebels against Rome were known as the Zealots and they are
described by Josephus as 'insurgents and crazy'. According to the Gospels,
Jesus in the early part of the first century had predicted that there would
be revolution in Judea:

> But when you see the desolating sacrilege set up where it ought not to be
> (let the reader understand), then let those who are in Judea flee to the moun-
> tains; let him who is on the house-top not go down, nor enter his house to
> take anything away, and let him who is in the field not turn back to take his
> mantle. And alas for those who are with child and for those who give suck
> in those days. Pray that it may not happen in winter. For in those days there
> will be such tribulation as has not been from the beginning of the creation
> which God created until now, and never will be. (Mark 13: 14–19)

In CE 66 the Zealots took control of Jerusalem and by CE 70 the city was
under Roman siege. On 6 August, the daily sacrifices in the Temple were
suspended and on 28 August the whole sanctuary went up in flames:

> The Roman legions charged in and no threat or reasonable argument could
> check their impulses; passion alone was in control . . . As they got near to
> the sanctuary, they pretended not to hear their leader's orders and they
> encouraged the men at the front to throw in more firebrands. The Zealots
> could do nothing to help; there was slaughter and flight everywhere . . . All
> around the altar the pile of dead bodies grew higher and higher and down
> the steps of the sanctuary there flowed a river of blood while the bodies of
> those butchered at the top slid down to the bottom. The soldiers were like

madmen: there was no stopping them and there could be no arguing with the fire. (Josephus, *The Jewish War* VI)

It was an appalling blow for the Jews:

> As the sages have said: When a man plasters his house, let him leave a small area unplastered to remind him of Jerusalem. Let a man prepare everything for a meal; then let him leave a small thing undone to remind him of Jerusalem. Let a woman put on all her finery and then let her take off one small thing, to remind her of Jerusalem. For it is said: If I forget thee O Jerusalem, may my right hand forget its cunning! (Tosefta, Sotah 15)

In the south the Zealots still held out against the Romans at the fortress of Masada. In CE 74, after a long siege, the Romans were on the point of conquest. Eleazar the rebel leader gathered his followers together and made an impassioned speech:

> My loyal followers, we decided long ago not to serve the Romans or anyone else. We only serve God, the true and righteous Lord of all men. Now the time has come to demonstrate our resolve by our actions. At a time like this we must not disgrace ourselves; we have never submitted to slavery in the past, even when slavery brought no danger. We must not choose it now . . . From the beginning, when we were first determined to claim our freedom . . . we should perhaps have read the mind of God and understood that his one Chosen People had been sentenced to extinction. If he had stayed gracious, or even only slightly angry with us, he would not have closed his eyes to the death of so many thousands, or permitted his Holy City to be burnt to the ground by the hand of his enemies . . . Come! While our hands are still free and can hold a sword, let us do a noble deed. Let us die unconquered by our enemies, and leave the world as free men together with our wives and children.
>
> When the Romans came upon the rows of corpses, they did not rejoice over their enemies, but they admired the nobility of their resolve and the way in which so many had shown, without trembling, complete contempt of death. (Josephus, *The Jewish War* VII)

Chronological Table

Circa BCE	Documents	Events in Jewish History
600–500	Nabonidus Chronicle; Cyrus Cylinder; Second Isaiah; Deuteronomic histories	Return from Babylonian Exile Temple rebuilt Persian domination
500–400	Haggai Malachi	Renewal under Ezra and Nehemiah
400–300	Samaritan Pentateuch; Ezra; Nehemiah; Ruth	Greek domination
300–200		Ptolemaic dynasty
200–100	Daniel	Selucid dynasty Maccabean revolt Hasmonean dynasty
100–0	I and II Maccabees	Roman domination Temple rebuilt
0–100	Josephus' *Antiquities* and *Jewish War*; Dead Sea Scrolls; New Testament	War against Rome Destruction of the Temple
100–200		
200–300	Mishnah; Tosefta	

Suggested Further Reading

The books of Ezra, Nehemiah, I and II Maccabees.

Josephus, *The Antiquities of the Jews*, London: Heinemann, 1926; and *The Jewish War*, ed. E. Mary Smallwood, trans. G. A. Williamson, New York: Viking Penguin, 1984.

G. Vermes, *The Dead Sea Scrolls in English*, New York: Viking Penguin, 1995.

G. Nicklesburg, *Jewish Literature between the Bible and the Mishnah*, London: SCM Press, 1981.

5

Rabbinic Judaism

1. The Academy at Javneh

The Pharisee Johanan ben Zakkai had managed to escape from Jerusalem during the siege. He settled in the town of Javneh and gathered around him a group of scholars (the Tannaim):

> Moses received the Torah on Mount Sinai and passed it on to Joshua, and Joshua to the elders, and the elders to the prophets and the prophets to the men of the Great Assembly . . . Simon the righteous was one of the last members of the Great Assembly . . . Antigonus of Solcho received the Torah from Simon the Righteous . . . Yose ben Yo'ezer of Zeredah and Yose ben Yohanan of Jerusalem received the Torah from them . . . Joshua ben Perahyah and Nittai the Arbelite received the Torah from them . . . Judah ben Tabbai and Simeon ben Shetah received the Torah from them . . . Shemayah and Avtalyon received the Torah from them . . . Hillel and Shammai received the Torah from them . . . Rabban Johanan ben Zakkai received the Torah from Hillel and Shammai; he used to say: If you have learned much Torah, do not give yourself any credit, for this was the purpose of your creation. (Mishnah, Avoth I)

Thus, despite the loss of the Temple, the great Pharisaic tradition of learning and interpretation was preserved:

> Simon the Righteous used to say: The world stands on three things – on the Torah, on the Temple service and on acts of kindness. (Mishnah, Avoth I)

But his successor, Rabbi Simeon, son of Gamaliel, could say:

> The world stands upon three things: upon justice, upon truth and upon peace. (Mishnah, Avoth I)

Within a generation, the Sanhedrin (Supreme Assembly), the Nasi

(Prince) and the Av Bet Din (Father of the Court) were re-established under Rabban Gamaliel II and Rabbi Joshua:

> When the Nasi comes in, all the people stand; they do not sit until he has told them to do so. When the Av Bet Din comes in, they stand on either side to make a passageway for him until he has come in and taken his place. (Talmud, Sanh VII)

> The Sanhedrin was arranged in a half circle so that everyone might see each other. The Nasi sat in the middle with the elders on his right and his left sides. R. Eleazar, the son of Zadok said: When Rabban Gamaliel sat at Javneh, my father and one other sat on his right and the other elders sat on his left. (Talmud, Sanh VIII)

The most distinguished scholar of the second century was perhaps Rabbi Akiva:

> R. Akiva used to say: Levity and joking encourage lewdness in a man; the tradition is a fence around the Torah; tithes are a fence around wealth; vows are a fence around abstinence; silence is a fence around wisdom . . . Everything is foreseen, but there is freedom of choice; the world is judged by grace, but all is according to the good or evil of works. (Mishnah, Avoth III)

Akiva became involved in another revolt against Rome, led by Simeon bar Kokhba (d. CE 135):

> Rabbi Johanan used to say: Our master used to expound, 'There shall come forth a star [Kokhab] out of Jacob [Numbers 24: 17], thus, do not read Kokhab [star] but Kozab [lie].' When Akiva saw bar Kokhba, he exclaimed, 'This is the king, the Messiah!' Rabbi Johanan b. Tortha retorted, 'Akiva, grass will grow in your cheeks and still the Messiah will not have come.' (Midrash, Lamentations R. II)

The history of the revolt is briefly recorded in Dio Cassius' *History of Rome*:

> [The Emperor Hadrian] founded a city named Aelia Capitolina in place of Jerusalem which had been burnt to the ground. On the site of the temple of the god, he built a new temple to Jupiter. This led to a war of no small import-ance or short duration, for the Jewish people thought it intolerable that for-eigners should be settled in their city and the worship of foreign gods to be held there . . . Five hundred and eighty thousand men were killed in the vari-

ous skirmishes and battles and there is no knowing how many died through famine, disease and fire. Thus nearly the whole of Judea was made desolate . . . Many wolves and hyenas rushed howling through the cities. (Dio Cassius, *History of Rome* LXIX)

Letters of bar Kokhba have survived. He appears to have been a dictatorial leader:

Simeon bar Kokhba to Jonathan and Masabala . . . all the men from Tekoa and the other places who are with you must be sent to me immediately. If you will not send them, be assured that you will be punished. (Bar Kokhba Letters)

He also seems to have been religiously observant. The following letter clearly refers to the celebration of Sukkot (the Feast of Tabernacles):

Simeon to Judah bar Menashe to Kiriath Araboya. I have sent you two donkeys. You will send two men with them to Jonathan bar Be'ayan and Masabala so that they pack up and send to the camp palm branches and citrons. From your place you must send others who will bring you myrtles and willows. See that they are set in order and send them on to the camp . . . Be well. (Ibid.)

Eventually bar Kokhba was killed at the siege of Bethar and Rabbi Akiva was flayed alive:

When Rabbi Akiva was taken out to be executed, it was time for the recital of the Shema, and while they tore at his flesh with iron combs, he was accepting upon himself the Kingdom of Heaven . . . He drew out the word 'ehad' [one] until he died while saying it. A voice from Heaven went forth and proclaimed: 'Happy are you Akiva, that your soul departed on the word "ehad" . . . Happy are you Akiva, that you are destined for the life of the World to Come.' (Talmud, Berakoth LXI)

After the Bar Kokhba Revolt, the Jews pursued a policy of conciliation with the Romans and the academy at Javneh was transferred to Galilee.

2. The Mishnah

From the second to the early fifth centuries, the Nasi was recognized by the Romans as the political head of the people of Judea:

We decree that all the privileges which our father, of blessed memory, and past emperors have conferred upon the eminent Patriarchs [Nasis] or upon those persons whom the Patriarchs have put in authority over others shall retain their full force. (Theodosian Canon XVI)

By the third Century the oral law was becoming increasingly complex. The Mishnah is an authoritative record of the debates and decisions of the Tannaim on various topics:

These are the ways in which the School of Shammai and the School of Hillel differ in the conduct of a meal. The School of Shammai first say the bene-diction for the day and then the benediction for the wine, whereas the School of Hillel first say the benediction for the wine and then the one for the day.

The School of Shammai say: First wash the hands and then mix the cup. The School of Hillel say: First mix the cup and then wash the hands.

The School of Shammai say: A man wipes his hands with a napkin and then lays it on the table, but the School of Hillel say: He lays it on a cush-ion. (Mishnah, Berakoth VIII)

The usual format is that the minority opinion is placed first followed by the accepted opinion:

If a man divorces his wife because of her bad reputation, he may not take her back; and if, because of a vow, he may not take her back. R. Judah says: If he divorced her because of a vow that many people know about, he may not take her back, but if only a few people know about it, then he may take her back. R. Meir says: He may not take her back if the vow needed the opinion of a sage to revoke, but for any vow that he could revoke himself he could take her back . . . R. Jose b. R. Judah said: Once in Sidon a man said to his wife, 'I will give everything away if I do not divorce you!' and he divorced her. But the sages allowed him to take her back as a precaution for the good of everyone. If a man divorces his wife because she is barren, R. Judah says: He may not take her back. But the Sages say: He may take her back. (Mishnah, Gittin IV)

Even though the Temple had been destroyed for more than a hundred years, the ritual of the sacrifices was remembered and recorded:

The lamb was not completely bound up; it was only tied . . . with its head to the south and its face to the west. He who was to slaughter it stood to the east facing west. The morning sacrifice took place in the north-west-ern corner of the second ring while the afternoon sacrifice was slaughtered at the north-eastern corner. He on whom the lot fell slaughtered it and he on whom the lot fell received the blood. He then came to the north-east corner and sprinkled the blood to the east and to the north and then he went to the south-east corner and sprinkled it to the east and to the south. The rest of the blood was poured out at the base of the altar on the south side. (Mishnah, Tamid IV)

Today the best known parts of the Mishnah are the ethical maxims:

Rabbi Johanan ben Zakkai said to his students: Go and find out the good way for a man to live. Rabbi Eleazar says: A good eye. Rabbi Joshua says: A good companion. Rabbi Jose says: A good neighbour. Rabbi Simeon says: Considering the results of one's actions. Rabbi Eleazar says: A good heart. He said to them: I prefer Eleazar ben Arakh's answer, because all your responses are included in his. (Mishnah, Avoth II)

R. Tarphon said: The day is long; the task is great; the labourers are idle; the wages are generous and the master of the house is pressing. (Mishnah, Avoth II)

There are four kinds of people who give to charity. One is willing to contribute himself, but he does not want others to give – he is jealous of what belongs to others. Another is willing that others give, but is unwilling to contribute himself – he is jealous of what belongs to himself. Then there is the one who both gives himself and wants others to give – he is a righteous man, and there is the man who neither gives himself nor wants others to give – he is wicked. (Mishnah, Avoth V)

Judah ben Tema used to say: Five is the age to start studying the scriptures; at ten the Mishnah can be begun; at thirteen we take on the yoke of the commandments; fifteen is the age to start studying the Talmud; eighteen is the time for marriage; at twenty a man should earn his own living; at thirty he has reached his physical prime; at forty he has achieved understanding; at fifty wisdom; at sixty old age, at seventy grey hairs, at eighty special strength; at ninety he is bent over and at one hundred he is as good as dead and gone from the world. (Mishnah, Avoth V)

The Mishnah was compiled by Judah Ha-Nasi (late second, early third century CE), generally referred to as Rabbi:

Rabbi studied thirteen different interpretations of his teaching, but he only taught R. Hiyya seven of them. Then Rabbi fell ill and R. Hiyya restored to his memory the seven versions which he had taught him, but the other six were lost. Now it happened that a certain fuller had overheard Rabbi when he was studying the lost six by himself; so R. Hiyya went to the fuller and learnt them from him and then repeated them back to Rabbi. (Talmud, Nedarim XLI)

Because Judah Ha-Nasi had enormous power and consorted with the Romans, he was not universally admired:

> Rabbi sent envoys to propose marriage to the widow (of R. Eleazar, son of R. Simeon). She sent back the message: Shall a basin which has held holy food be used for profane purposes? (Talmud, Babu Mezia LXXXIV)

However, his learning and sanctity were undisputed:

> At the time of his dying, Rabbi raised ten fingers to Heaven and said, 'Lord of the Universe, you know and it has been revealed to you that I have laboured in the study of the Torah with my ten fingers and that I did not enjoy any worldly advantage even with my little finger. May there be peace in my resting place, according to your will.' A voice from Heaven echoed, saying, 'He shall enter into peace.' (Talmud, Kethuboth CIV)

3. Rabbinic Interpretation of Scripture

The Tannaim were also preoccupied with the interpretation of the biblical text. Such interpretation is known as 'midrash'. Some midrash simply amplify and explain biblical passages:

> Then God said, 'Let us make man in our image.' (Genesis 1: 26)

> Midrash: With whom did God take counsel? R. Joshua b. Levi said: He consulted all the works of Heaven and earth, like a king who has two counsellors whom he consults over everything. R. Samuel b. Nahman said: He consulted with the works of each day, like a king who has an adviser on whom he totally depends. R. Ammi said: He consulted his own heart like a king who has a palace built for him by an architect, but if the palace does not please him, then the person he is annoyed with is the architect. (Genesis R. VIII)

> The woman said to the serpent, 'We may eat of the fruit of the trees of the garden.' (Genesis 3: 2)

> Midrash: Now where was Adam during this conversation? Abba Halfon b. Konah said: After he had engaged in sexual congress, he had fallen asleep. The Rabbis said: God took him and was leading him around the world, suggesting to him that this was a suitable place for planting trees and there was a good place for sowing seed. (Genesis R. XIX)

And the Lord put a mark on Cain. (Genesis 4: 15)

Midrash: R. Judah said: He caused the orb of the sun to shine for him. R. Nehemiah said to him: He would not cause the orb of the sun to shine for that villain. No! He caused leprosy to break out all over him . . . Rav said: He gave him a dog. Abba Jose said: He caused a horn to grow out of him. Rav said: He made him into an example for murderers. R. Hanin said: He made him into an example for the penitent. R. Levi said on behalf of R. Simeon b. Lakish: He suspended judgement until the Flood came and swept him away. (Genesis R. XXII)

Other midrash use a scriptural text to explain a custom or to support a theological position:

Put off your shoes from your feet for the place on which you are standing is holy ground. (Exodus 3: 5)

Midrash: Wherever the Divine Presence appears, a man must not go about wearing shoes; we find the same in the case of Joshua: 'Put off your shoes' [Joshua 5: 15]. This is why the priests in the Temple ministered barefooted. (Exodus R. II)

Write these words; in accordance with these words I have made a covenant with you and with Israel. (Exodus 34: 27)

Midrash: When God revealed himself at Sinai to give the Torah to Israel, he gave it to Moses in order – Bible, Mishnah, Talmud . . . 'Write these words' refers to the Bible; 'in accordance with these words' applies to the Mishnah and Talmud which keep Israel separate from the heathen. (Exodus R. XXIV)

The Gospels record that Jesus made use of similar techniques of biblical interpretation when arguing that the dead were resurrected:

Have you not read in the book of Moses, in the passage about the bush [Exodus 3: 6], how God said to him, 'I am the God of Abraham and the God of Isaac and the God of Jacob.' He is not God of the dead, but of the living. (Mark 12: 27)

In the second century CE, Rabbi Ishmael expounded thirteen rules of biblical exegesis. These include:

1. Inference from a less important to a more important case . . . Since the daily offering . . . overrides the Sabbath, then is it not logical that the Passover

offering . . . will override the Sabbath?

2. Inference from an identical word or phrase. 'Be-mo'ado' [In its set time] is stated in connection with the Passover and . . . in connection with the daily sacrifice. A 'Be-mo'ado' . . . with the daily sacrifice overrides the Sabbath so 'Be-mo'ado' . . . with the Passover overrides the Sabbath . . .

3. Construction of a general principle from one verse and from two verses. 'If he knocks out the tooth of his slave' [Exodus 21: 27] could be understood to mean either a milk tooth or a permanent tooth, but scripture also says, 'When a man strikes the eye of a slave and destroys it' [Exodus 21: 26]. Just as the eye is an organ which does not grow back again, so too must the tooth be one which does not grow back again . . .

4. General and specific . . . Rava objected: If it had just said, 'When any man of you brings an offering to the Lord, you shall bring your offering of cattle ['behamah', Leviticus 1: 2], I would agree that wild creatures are included in the category behamah . . . but the text goes on to state 'from the herd or from the flock' [Leviticus 1: 2]; so sacrifices of the herd and flock have been commanded, not of the wild beasts . . .

13. Two contradictory passages stand as they are until a third passage can be found to decide between them. R. Akiva says: One passage says: 'You shall offer the Passover sacrifice to the Lord your God from the flock ['zon'] or the herd, ['vaqar', Deuteronomy 16: 2], and another says: 'You shall take it from the sheep ['kevasim'] or from the goats, ['izzim', Exodus 12: 5]. How can both these verses stand . . . ? Now the passage: 'Select lambs [zon] for yourself according to your families' [Exodus 12: 21] decides in this instance since it demonstrates that only from the flock [zon] . . . can the Passover offering come. (R. Ishmael, Mekhilta, Pisha 4)

4. The Academies

The Sages maintained that the academies in which the oral law was debated originated in biblical times:

R. Hama b. Hanina said: Our ancestors were never left without the Scholars' Council. In Egypt they had the Scholars' Council, as it is said: Go and gather the elders of Israel together [Exodus 3: 16]; in the desert they had the Scholars' Council, as it is said: Gather for me seventy men of the elders of Israel [Numbers 11: 16]; our father Abraham was an elder and a member of the Scholars' Council. (Talmud, Yoma XXVIII)

Many stories were told of the academies in the days of Hillel and Shammai before the Destruction of the Temple (see Chapter 5, Part 1):

Our rabbis taught: The house of Shammai and the house of Hillel were in dispute for two and a half years. The house of Shammai insisted that it would have been better if man had never been created while the House of Hillel maintained that it was better that he was created than that he never had been made. They finally took a vote. (Talmud, 'Erubim XIII)

After the destruction, when the Sanhedrin (see Chapter 5, Part 1) had been re-established, other scholars founded their own academies throughout the land of Israel and beyond:

Follow the scholars to their academies: R. Eliezer to Lydda, R. Johanan b. Zakkai to Beror Hail, R. Joshua to Peki'in, Rabban Gamaliel to Jabneh, R. Akiva to Benai Berak, R. Jose to Sepphoris, R. Judah b. Bathyra to Nisibis, R. Joshua to the Exile, Rabbi to Beth She'arim. (Talmud, Sanhedrin XXXII)

The purpose of the academies was to instruct students in Torah and to interpret the oral law:

There will come a time when a man will look for one of the laws of the Torah and will not find it, or one of the laws of the rabbis, and will not find it . . . Then they will say, 'Let us start with Hillel and Shammai.' (Tosefta, Eduyoth I)

The Sanhedrin in Palestine, presided over by the Nasi (see Chapter 5, Part 1) held the greatest authority, particularly with respect to setting the calendar and the order of the liturgy:

Once Rabban Gamaliel went to have his authority confirmed by the Governor of Syria and it was a long time before he returned. So they declared the year a leap year, conditional on the approval of Rabban Gamaliel. When he did return, he said, 'I approve', so the year was counted as a leap year. (Mishnah, Eduyoth 7: 7)

Our rabbis taught: Simeon ha-Pakuli arranged the order of the Eighteen Benedictions before Rabban Gamaliel at Javneh. (Talmud, Berakoth XXVIII)

After the Mishnah had been compiled by Judah Ha-Nasi, its interpreters in the academies were known collectively as the Amoraim (spokesmen):

How are we to explain the phrase 'the weighing up of opinions?' R. Papa answered: If two Tannaim and two Amoraim are on opposing sides, and it is not stated explicitly whose side is correct, if a ruling is made in accordance with one set of opinions, but the general practice follows the other – this is a case of the erroneous weighing up of opinions. (Talmud, Sanhedrin XXXIII)

Rav said: Four deductions seem to follow from the Mishnah, but he was only completely sure of three. (Talmud, Kiddushin LII)

At the end of every discussion, a vote of all the scholars was taken:

[Where] one permits and one prohibits, [where] one declares levitically unclean and one declares clean and where all say: We have not heard a tradition concerning this. In these cases a vote is taken. (Tosefta, Sanhedrin VII)

Head of each academy was a Rosh Yeshivah:

R. Joseph was 'Sinai' [encyclopaedic in his knowledge of the Torah] while Rabbah was an 'uprooter of mountains' [skilful in argument]. When the time came that one should be Rosh Yeshivah, they sent to ask: Who should be preferred, Sinai or the Uprooter of Mountains. The answer came back: Sinai, because everyone needs to know the authentic traditions. But R. Joseph would not accept the position . . . so Rabbah remained Rosh Yeshivah for twenty-two years. (Talmud, Berakoth LXIV)

Outside Palestine, the academies associated with Rav at Sura and Samuel at Nehardia were particularly famous:

'Our rabbis in Babylon' refer to Rav and Samuel. 'Our rabbis in the land of Israel' to R. Abba. (Talmud, Sanhedrin XVII)

During this period, the day-to-day affairs of the Jewish community in Babylon were in the hands of the Exilarch, a government-appointed official:

Our teacher [R. Judah Ha-Nasi] was very modest and he used to say: . . . If Huna, the Resh Galuta [the Head of the Exile/Exilarch] were to come to this place, I would stand up for him, for he is descended from Judah whereas I am descended from Benjamin. He is descended on the male side and I on the female side. (Midrash, Genesis R. XXXIII)

The heads of the Babylonian academies (the Gaonim) were initially subordinate to the Exilarch, but they later asserted their independence. At the end of the third century, the academy at Pumbedita was founded as a successor to Nehardia:

Rabina said: I visited Meremar at Sura. When the deputy of the congregation went down and recited it [the kiddush prayer] in the manner of the elders of Pumbedita, everyone tried to silence him, but he said to them, 'Leave him alone; the Law is as declared by the elders of Pumbedita.' (Talmud, Pesahim CXVII)

The title 'Rabbi' was only used for those who had been ordained, and ordination was limited to teachers living in the land of Israel:

R. Joshua b. Levi said: There is no ordination outside Palestine . . . R. Johanan was distressed when R. Shaman b. Abba was not with him to receive ordination. (Talmud, Sanhedrin XIV)

Consequently, the teachers of the Babylonian academies took the title of 'Rav'.

5. The Talmud

The Jerusalem Talmud was compiled at the end of the fourth century CE and the Babylonian Talmud during the sixth century CE. Both record the discussions (Gemara) of the Amoraim on the Mishnah and are vast compendia of law, theology, ethics, etiquette, legend and magic. Only the briefest samples can be given to convey the flavour of the whole:

Mishnah: The main kinds of work are forty minus one.
Gemara: Why is the number stated? R. Johanan said: So that if a man performs them all in a single state of ignorance, he is guilty on account of each one separately. (Talmud, Shabbath LXXIII)

Again they sat and thought: Concerning what we have learned, the main kinds of work are forty minus one – to what do they correspond?
R. Hanina b. Hama said to them: To the forms of work in the Tabernacle.
R. Jonathan son of R. Eleazar said: Thus R. Simeon b. R. Jose b. Lakonia used to say: They correspond to 'work', 'his work' and 'the work of', which can be found forty times minus one in the Torah.
R. Joseph asked: Is the verse 'And he went into the house to do work' [Genesis 39: 11] to be included in this total or not?
Abbaye answered him: Bring out the scroll of the Law and we will count!
Rabbah b. Bar Hanina used to say in R. Johanan's name: They did not move from there until they brought a scroll of the Law and counted. (Talmud, Shabbath XLIX)

R. Shimi b. Ukba was often in the company of R. Simeon b. Pazzi . . . He said to him: What does the verse 'Bless the Lord O my soul, and all that is within me bless His Holy Name?' [Psalms 103: 1] mean? He answered: Come and see how the abilities of human beings fall short of the abilities of the Holy One, blessed be He. A human being is capable of drawing a figure on a wall, but he cannot animate it with breath or spirit, bowels or intestines. But the Holy One, blessed be He, is not like that. He shapes one form in the middle of another and gives it breath and spirit, bowels and intestines . . . It is the nature of flesh and blood to be outlived by its works, but the Holy One, blessed be He, outlives all His works. (Talmud, Berakoth X)

R. Johanan said: The Holy One, blessed be He, makes a proclamation every day about three things: a bachelor who lives in a large town without committing sin, a poor man who restores lost property to its owner and a rich man who tithes his produce secretly . . . The Holy One, blessed be He, loves three kinds of people: he who does not lose his temper, he who does not get drunk and he who does not stand upon his rights. The Holy One, blessed be He, hates three kinds of people: he who says one thing with his lips and another in his heart, he who has evidence supporting his neighbour, but does not testify for him and he who sees something indecent in his neighbour and testifies alone against him. (Talmud, Pesahim CXIII)

R. Hanan b. Rabbah said: Everyone knows why a bride goes under the bridal canopy, but anyone who speaks lewdly about it, even if he has been marked for a sentence of seventy years happiness, that sentence will be reversed. (Talmud, Shabbath XXXIII)

Rav Judah said in the name of Rav: When Moses went up on high, he found the Holy One, blessed be He, fixing small strokes like crowns to the letters. Moses said: Lord of the Universe, why is this necessary?

He answered: After many generations a man will arise named Akiva b. Joseph, who will explain upon each stroke masses and masses of Law.

Moses said: Lord of the Universe, let me see him.

He answered: Turn around.

Moses went and sat down at the back behind eight rows of disciples. He was not able to follow the arguments and he was uneasy. Then they came to a certain subject and the disciples said to their master: How do you know that?

The master answered: It is a Law given to Moses on Mount Sinai.

And Moses felt better. Then he returned to the Holy One, blessed be He, and said: Lord of the Universe, even though you had such a man, you gave the Torah by me!

He replied: Be quiet, for that was my decree.

Then Moses said: Lord of the Universe, you have shown me his Torah, now show me his reward.

He said: Turn round.

Moses turned round and he saw men weighing out Akiva's flesh on the market stalls. Moses cried: Lord of the Universe, such Torah and such a reward!

He answered: Be quiet, for that is my decree. (Talmud, Menahoth XXIX)

Rav Judah said in Rav's name: The Holy One, blessed be He, did not create a single thing in all his world which has no purpose. He created the snail as a remedy for a scab; the fly as an antidote to the hornet; the mosquito [crushed] for a serpent [bite]; a serpent as a remedy for a boil and a [crushed] spider as a remedy for a scorpion [sting]. A serpent is a remedy for a boil. What is the treatment? One black and white serpent should be taken, boiled to a pulp and then rubbed in. (Talmud, Shabbath LXXVII)

Chronological Table

Circa CE	Documents	Events in Jewish History
0–100	Mark's Gospel	Destruction of the Temple Establishment of academy at Javneh
100–200	bar Kokhba Letters; R. Ishmael's Mekhilta	Bar Kokhba Revolt Era of the Tannaim
200–300	Midrash; Mishnah; Cassius' *History of Rome*	Compilation of Mishnah
300–400	Jerusalem Talmud	Era of Amoraim
400–500	Theodosian Canon	Era of Amoraim Compilation of Babylonian Talmud
500–600	Babylonian Talmud	

Suggested Further Reading

H. Freedman and M. Simon, eds. *Midrash Rabbah* (10 vols.), London: Soncino, 1939.

H. Danby, trans., *Mishnah*, Oxford: Oxford University Press, 1933.

I. Epstein, ed., *Babylonian Talmud*, London: Soncino, 1948.

H. L. Strack, *Introduction to the Talmud and Midrash*, trans. M. Bockmuehl and J. Neusner, Minneapolis, MA: Fortress Press, 1992.

6

The Dispersion

1. Jews in the Roman Empire

By the first century CE, there were Jewish communities throughout the Roman empire:

> Now Paul and his company set sail from Paphos and came to Perga in Pamphylia . . . and came to Antioch of Pisidia. And on the Sabbath day they went to the synagogue and sat down . . . Now at Iconium they entered together into the Jewish synagogue . . . Now when they had passed through Amphipolis and Apollonia, they came to Thessalonica where there was a synagogue of the Jews . . . Now when Paul was waiting for them at Athens . . . he argued in the synagogue with the Jews . . . After this he left Athens and went to Corinth . . . and he argued in the synagogue every Sabbath . . . And so we came to Rome . . . After three days he called together the local leaders of the Jews. (Acts 13: 13–14; 14: 1; 17: 1, 16–17; 18: 1, 4; 28: 14, 17)

It seems that the Jews enjoyed certain legal privileges in the Roman empire:

> We order that priests, rulers of the synagogues, fathers of the synagogues and all others who serve the synagogues shall be free from compulsory public service. (Theodosian Canon)

During this period many individuals seem to have been attracted to synagogue worship (these were known as God-fearers) and some underwent full conversion:

> On the Sabbath day they went to the synagogue and sat down . . . So Paul stood up and motioning with his hand said, 'Men of Israel, and you who fear God, listen . . . Brethren, sons of the family of Abraham and those among you that fear God.' (Acts 13: 14, 16, 26)

> Then said Jesus to the crowds . . . 'Woe to you Scribes and Pharisees, hypocrites! For you traverse sea and land to make a single proselyte, and

when he becomes a proselyte, you make him twice as much a child of hell as yourselves.' (Matthew 23: 1, 15)

The convert who has come of his own free will is dearer to God than all the hordes of Israelites who stood at Mount Sinai. This is because the Israelites would not have accepted the Torah if they had not witnessed the thunder, lightning, erupting mountain and sounded trumpets. But the convert saw none of these things and still came and gave himself up to the Holy One, blessed be He, and accepted the yoke of Heaven. Who can be dearer to God than this man? (Midrash, Tanh. B. VI)

Those who want to become converts for love of a Jew or a Jewess are not accepted. Nor are they accepted if they are converting from fear or for worldly advantage. But Rav said: They are to be accepted; this is the Law: they are to be considered as converts and they are not to be put off, as would-be converts are put off at the outset. They must receive friendly treatment because it may be, after all, that they have pure motives. (Jerusalem Talmud, Kiddushin IV)

Even before the rise of Christianity there were occasional outbursts of anti-Semitism in the ancient world:

The other customs of the Jews are abominable and low and owe their survival to their depravity . . . they are very loyal to each other and are always ready to show compassion, but they feel only hate and hostility towards other people. They sit separately at meals and sleep separately and, although as a people they are prone to lust, they will not have intercourse with foreign women . . . Those who are converted to their ways follow the same practice and the first lesson they learn is to despise the gods, disown their native land and to regard their parents, siblings and children as being of no importance. (Tacitus, *Histories*, Book 5)

The emerging Christian Church portrayed the Jews as the murderers of Jesus and perceived mainstream Judaism as corrupt:

Now at the feast the governor was accustomed to release for the crowd any one prisoner whom they wanted. And they then had a notorious prisoner called Barabbas. So when they had gathered, Pilate said to them, 'Whom do you want me to release for you, Barabbas or Jesus who is called Christ?' and they said, 'Barabbas.' Pilate said to them, 'Then what shall I do with Jesus who is called Christ?' They all said, 'Let him be crucified.' And he said, 'Why, what evil has he done?' But they shouted all the more, 'Let him be crucified.' So when Pilate saw that he was gaining nothing, but rather that a riot was beginning, he took water and washed his hands before the crowd, saying, 'I am innocent of this man's blood. See to it yourselves.' And all the people answered, 'His blood be on us and on our children.' (Matthew 27: 15–17, 21–5)

And they stirred up the people and the elders and the scribes and they came upon him and seized him and brought him before the Council . . . And Stephen said . . . 'You stiff-necked people, uncircumcised in heart and ears, you always resist the Holy Spirit. As your fathers did, so do you. Which of the prophets did not your fathers persecute? And they killed those who announced beforehand the coming of the Righteous One, whom you have now betrayed and murdered, you who received the Law as delivered by angels and did not keep it . . .' Then they cast him out of the city and stoned him. (Acts, 6: 12; 7: 1, 51–3, 58)

Once Christianity had been adopted as the official religion of the Roman empire, the position of Jews changed dramatically for the worse.

2. Jews under Early Islamic rule

Many of the early Christian Fathers were virulently anti-Semitic:

I call on Heaven and earth as witnesses against you if anyone should attend their Feast of the blowing of trumpets, or share in their fasts or in their observance of the Sabbath or indeed observe any important or trivial rule of the Jews. I will be innocent of your blood.' (John Chrysostom, *Against the Jews* 1)

Babylonia was outside the influence of the Christianity of the Roman empire. However, there was another threat. In the seventh century CE the Prophet Muhammad claimed to have received a revelation from Allah, the one true God, which superseded the messages given to Abraham and Moses:

You people of the book, why do you dispute so about Abraham, since the Torah and the Gospels were given after his time? Why don't you use your reason? You are always prepared to discuss things that you understand, why do you insist on arguing about matters of which you know nothing? Knowledge belongs to God – you do not have it. Abraham was not a Jew, nor was he a Christian. He was a true worshipper and a Muslim . . .
It is said that you must be a Jew or a Christian to be rightly guided. Instead you should say, 'The community of Abraham is ours. He was not a polytheist, he was a true worshipper.' Say, 'We believe in God and what he has revealed to us, and what he revealed to Abraham, Ishmael, Isaac, Jacob and the tribes, as well as what was shown to Moses, to Jesus and to the prophets from their Lord. We do not distinguish between any of them and

we make submission only to God.' If they believe this faith of yours, then they are rightly guided but if they turn away, then they are clearly in schism. God the all-hearing and all-knowing will guide you in all your dealings with them. (Qur'án, Sura 2, 3)

Initially Muhammad seems to have hoped that the Jews would join his movement:

Asishah reported: The Jews came to the Prophet (may the blessings and peace of Allah be upon him) and said, 'May death overtake you!' Asishah retorted, 'And you too! And may Allah curse you and may Allah's fury come down upon you!' But the Prophet said, 'Gently Asishah! Be courteous and keep away from harshness!' (Hadith, Bukhari 78)

When it became clear that the Jews were not going to accept Islam, Muhammad's attitude became more negative:

Long ago we made a covenant with the people of Israel and we sent message to them. Each time a messenger came with a message that they did not like, they would say some of the messengers were liars and they would murder others. They imagined that nothing evil would come out of it and in this way they grew deaf and blind. (Qur'án, Sura 5)

Islam spread largely by conquest and by the start of the eighth century CE North Africa, Syria, Egypt, Persia and Babylonia were part of the new empire. Under the pact of Omar (c. 800) the Jewish religion was tolerated, although Jews faced certain civil disabilities such as being compelled to pay a special poll tax and having to wear distinctive clothes. These provisions are in accordance with the teachings of the Qur'án:

Fight those who do not believe in Allah, or in the Last Day, or who disregard things forbidden by Allah and his Apostle, or who do not acknowledge the true religion. Even though they are the People of the Book, they must pay the special poll tax in token of their willing submission. (Qur'án, Sura 9)

Nonetheless, the Muslim leaders supported the Jewish institutions of Babylon and even confirmed the authority of the Exilarch and the Gaonim (see Chapter 5, Parts 4 and 5):

At this time Omar ben Akatif [Caliph 634–644] appeared. He conquered Syria, Philistia, Damascus, Egypt and the whole of Palestine including Jerusalem. He also fought against the King of the Persians, Yazdegerd; he conquered his whole country and took his wives and his children into captivity. And Omar gave one of Yazdegerd's daughters to the Exilarch, Bustani, to be his wife. And when she was married, she left her people and her faith and he loved her very much. (Joseph HaCohen, *The Vale of Tears*)

The following is an account of the splendour of the Exilarchate in the twelfth century CE:

There are about forty thousand Jews in Baghdad and they dwell in comfort, prosperity and respect under the great Caliph . . . At the head of them all is Daniel, son of Hisdai, who has the title of 'Our Master, the Head of the Exile of all Israel'. He has a book of family trees going back as far as King David of Israel. The Jews call him 'Our Master, Head of the Exile' while the Muslims call him 'Noble Son of David' and he has been given authority over all the congregations of Israel . . . Every Thursday he goes to visit the great Caliph escorted by horsemen – non-Jews as well as Jews – and heralds announce before him, 'Make way before our Master, the noble son of David' . . . He appears before the Caliph and kisses his hand and the Caliph stands and places him on a throne which Muhammad ordered to be made in his honour. (*The Voyages of Benjamin of Tudela*)

Jewish merchants traded throughout the Muslim empire and beyond. In consequence of their activities, according to legend, in the ninth century the King of the Khazars was converted to Judaism:

The King of the Khazars, as we know from the histories, became a convert to the Jewish religion about four hundred years ago. He had a dream in which it seemed that an angel spoke to him, saying, 'Your way of thinking is certainly pleasing to the Creator, but your actions are not pleasing.' However, he was so devoted to the Khazar religion that he consecrated himself with a perfect heart to the temple services and sacrifices. Despite this devotion, one night the angel came again and said, 'This way of thinking is pleasing to God, but not this way of behaving.' This caused the King to think about the different religions and creeds and he finally became a convert to Judaism together with many of his tribe. (Judah Halevy, *The Kuzari*)

3. Karaism

During the course of Jewish history, various groups have rejected the oral interpretations of the rabbis:

And Saduccees came to him, who say there is no resurrection. (Mark 12: 18)

Furthermore they pollute the Holy Spirit with their mouths, they speak blasphemies against the laws of God's covenant, saying, 'They are not sure.' They say abominations about them, 'Behold, all you who kindle a fire, who set brands alight' [Isaiah 50: 11], 'They hatch adders' eggs, they weave the spider's web' [Isaiah 59: 5]. (Damascus Document found among the Dead Sea Scrolls)

The Karaites who first emerged in the eighth century CE shared this tradition:

We are not compelled to follow the customs of our forefathers in every respect, but we must think about their ways and compare their behaviour and their laws with the words of the Torah. If we find that the teachings of our forefathers do correspond exactly to scripture, then we must accept them and listen to them. We must follow them; we must not change them. But if their teachings are different from those of scripture, we must reject them and must look for ourselves and investigate and ponder the commandments of the Torah for ourselves. What is written down in the Law of Moses (peace be unto him) about the commandments and other matters does not need any sign or witness to demonstrate its truth; but what is handed down from our forefathers needs both proof and a responsible witness. (Sahl ben Mazliah, *An Open Rebuke*)

Different accounts are given of the origin of the movement's founder, Anan ben David. The first extract was written by a Karaite scholar a thousand years after the event, in the eighteenth century, while the second comes from a champion of the rabbis:

Anan the Pious had been appointed Judge and Exilarch of all the Jews in the Arab empire, by the agreement of the Arab King and the Jewish people. He wrapped himself in a cloak of zeal and was very jealous for the Lord of Hosts, the God of Israel, and for his true and perfect Torah which had for so many years been in the possession of the Pharisees. He wanted to restore the crown of the Law to its former glory so he began to preach in public and to argue against the Mishnah, the oral law, and to deny it and to reject it utterly. When the whole congregation of Pharisees saw and heard all this, these accursed villains met together and rebelled against him and plotted to murder him. (Isaac Luzki, *The Path of the Righteous*)

Anan had a younger brother called Hananiah. Although Anan was older in age and had a greater understanding of the Torah, the sages of that time were unwilling to elect him as Exilarch because of his persistent unruliness and irreverence which were an inherent part of his character. So the sages chose Hananiah his brother, who was exceedingly modest and shy and who feared God greatly, and made him Exilarch. Then Anan was furious together with every scoundrel who still held the Sadducean and Boethusian opinion and he decided to cause a schism because he was frightened of the government of the time. These heretics appointed Anan as their Exilarch. (? Saadiah Gaon, *The Refutation of Anan*)

Since there was such emphasis in Karaite theology on individual opinion, there were many different groups of Karaites:

> The rabbis believe that their laws and rulings have been passed down by the prophets; if this is so, there should exist no differences of opinion among them and the fact that there are such differences shows that their arrogant belief is false. We, however, reach our views through reason and reason can lead to a variety of conclusions. (Jacob al-Kirkisani, *Book of Lights*)

Karaite communities were established in Egypt, North Africa, Persia and Israel. The Karaites who settled in Israel were particularly famous for their biblical scholarship:

> With the Karaites, the correct understanding of the book of God increased. People came from the east and from the west and commitment to religion and the desire for knowledge grew ever greater. They wanted to live in Jerusalem so they left the comfort of their homes and lived in the world as ascetics . . . They are the lilies, and the pious who have clung to the teaching of the book will be numbered among them. (Salman b. Jeruhim, *Explanation of Psalm* 69)

> Concerning the Jews, both the Asma'ath [Rabbanites], who are the vast majority, and the Ananites [Karaites] who believe in righteousness and the one God, in their interpretation of the Hebrew books, the Torah, the Prophets and the Psalms [which make up the twenty-four books] and in their translations into Arabic, rely on a number of Jews who are greatly respected and most of whom we have met personally including Abu Kather Yahya b. Zakariya [probably the Karaite, Yehuda Ha-Nazir] . . . and Said b. Yaqub al-Faiyumi [probably the Rabbanite, Saadiah Gaon]. (al-Masudi, *Library of Arab Geography*)

Among the most famous of these Karaite biblical scholars was Ben Asher in the ninth century, of whose biblical manuscript Moses Maimonides the philosopher wrote:

> Everyone relies on this book because it was corrected and its details were fixed by Ben Asher over a period of many years. It is said that he corrected it many times and I have relied on it. (Moses Maimonides, *Mishneh Torah*)

Later Karaite communities were set up in the Crimea, in Poland and Lithuania, of which some survive to this day. In the nineteenth century the Karaites of Russia achieved the status of 'Russian Karaites of the Old Testament Faith' and thus avoided the civil disabilities imposed on Jews (see Chapter 11, Part 2). They also escaped the Holocaust since the Nazis believed their 'racial psychology' was not Jewish (see Chapter 12, Part 2). Nonetheless, in recent years they have been persecuted in Arab states and a sizeable group has settled in the State of Israel under the Law of Return (see Chapter 13, Part 4).

4. The Golden Age of Spanish Jewry

Islamic Spain between the tenth and twelfth centuries CE was the scene of a flowering of Jewish culture. Some members of the community, such as Hasdai ibn Shaprut even became prominent officials of the secular government:

> Praise be to the all-kindly God for the extent of his mercy towards me! Kings of the earth who know of Caliph Abd-al-Rahman's splendour and power bring gifts to him, using expensive presents to curry his favour – kings such as the King of the Franks, the King of the Germans, the King of Constantinople and others. All these presents pass through my hands and I am responsible for sending gifts in return. May the words of my mouth give praise to the God of Heaven who bestows his loving kindness onto me – not through any merit of my own, but through his overflowing mercy. (Hasdai ibn Shaprut, letter to the King of the Khazars)

Another powerful Jewish statesman was Samuel ha-Levi who was given the honorary title of 'ha-Nagid' (the Prince):

> Rabbi Samuel ha-Levi was appointed Nagid in the year 4787 [CE 1023] and he greatly helped the Jews of Spain, of north-west and north-central Africa, of Egypt, of Sicily, and even those who lived as far away as the Babylonian academy and the Holy City of Jerusalem. He helped all the students who lived in those lands, even those as far away as the Babylonian Academy and the Holy City of Jerusalem. All the students who lived in those lands gained from his generosity because he purchased many copies of the Holy Scriptures, the Mishnah and the Talmud . . . He spread the knowledge of the Torah far and wide and he died at a ripe old age, having won four crowns – the crown of Torah, the crown of high rank, the crown of Levitical descent and, most important of all, the crown of a good name acquired through his good deeds. (Abraham ibn Daud, *The Line of Tradition*)

At the same time Solomon ibn Gabirol was at work. His philosophical writings were later used by the Christian Franciscans and many of his hymns have become part of the synagogue liturgy:

> I beg and beseech thee, O my God,
> Remember the sorrows that come upon us.
> If I have done evil in my life,
> Do good to me at my final end.
> Do not return measure for measure
> To us whose sins are measureless
> And whose death is an unhappy ending.
> (Solomon ibn Gabirol, *Royal Crown*)

In 1146 a new, less tolerant, Muslim dynasty took over southern Spain and many Jews fled north where they were encouraged by the Christian kings to settle. Some of the exiles found their new home sadly uncivilized:

> I am like a gentleman among barbarians,
> Like a lion among a colony of parrots and monkeys.
> (Moses ben Ezra, *Poems*)

Nevertheless, in the early days the Jewish community of Christian Spain enjoyed a measure of security:

> Jews are a nation who, although they do not accept the religion of our Lord Jesus Christ, yet the great Christian kings have always allowed them to live among them . . . Jews should live their lives quietly and discreetly among Christians, following their own religious practices and not slandering the faith of our Lord Jesus Christ in which Christians believe . . . Because a synagogue is a place where God's name is worshipped, we forbid any Christians to vandalize it, or steal anything from it or remove anything by force (except if a criminal seeks sanctuary there) . . . In addition we prohibit any Christian from putting an animal in a synagogue, or loitering in it or putting any obstruction in the way of the Jews when they are holding their services according to the beliefs. (Code of Alfonso X)

Among the poets of this later period was the philosopher Judah Halevy (see also Chapter 7, Part 3):

> Let us never forget the Sabbath day,
> Let it be kept by us as a foretaste of eternal peace;
> Just as Noah's dove found its rest on the day
> Let all who are exhausted be refreshed.
> At Mount Sinai the covenant was affirmed,
> With a single voice they vowed to obey.

For the Lord is our God, the Lord is One,
Blessed is he who gives rest to the weary.
(Judah Halevy, *Poems*)

Several codifiers, including Maimonides (see also Chapter 7, Part 4) produced summaries of the Jewish law:

> There are eight levels in the giving of charity, each one higher than the other.
> The highest level . . . is to help a Jew who has been crushed by giving him
> a gift or by taking him into partnership or by finding such work for him
> that he is put back on his feet and no longer depends on charity . . . The
> second level is the man who gives charity to the poor. He does not know
> to whom he is giving while the recipient does not know from whom he is
> receiving . . . the third level is when the donor knows the recipient, but the
> poor man does not know the donor . . . the fourth level is when the poor
> man knows from whom he is receiving, but the donor does not know to
> whom he is giving . . . the fifth level is when a man gives even before he is
> asked . . . the sixth level is when a man gives after he has been asked . . .
> the seventh level is when a man gives less than he should, but gives graciously
> and at the lowest level is the man who gives reluctantly. (Moses Maimonides,
> Mishneh Torah)

By this time the famous academies of Sura and Pumbedita (see Chapter 5,
Part 4) had declined in prestige and consequently Spanish authorities felt
free to issue Responsa to legal questions which arose in their community:

> My last word is that each case must be judged on its own merits, for the
> correct application of the Law depends on the virtuous intention of the heart.
> Our Torah, which is true, upholds truth above every other consideration so
> the judge must make up his mind in accordance with the truth. (Solomon
> ibn Adret, *Responsa*)

5. Jews in Christian Europe

The early Jewish communities of Europe were self-contained units and
by the tenth century CE there were important centres of Jewish learning
in northern France and the Rhineland. Pre-eminent was the towering
figure of Rashi (Solomon ben Isaac of Troyes), who produced commentaries on all the books of the Bible and all the tractates of the Talmud:

> Leviticus 24: 19–20: When a man causes a disfigurement in his neighbour,
> as he has done, so it shall be put in him, fracture for fracture, eye for eye,
> tooth for tooth.

It shall be done to him: our rabbis have explained that this does not mean putting a real disfigurement on him, but that he should be compensated for the injury with money. This is done by assessing the injury as one would with a slave who has been hurt. The proof for this is to be found in the word 'put' – which implies that something, namely money, is 'put' from one hand into another. (Rashi, *Commentary*)

Nevertheless, Jewish existence was perilous in Europe. Many were slaughtered during the First Crusade:

The wicked Emico, the Jews' enemy, came with his whole army against the gate of the city and the citizens let him in. Then the enemies of the Lord said to one another: 'Look, they have opened the city gate for us. We can avenge the blood of the Crucified One.' The children of the Holy Covenant still clung to their Creator although they saw the enormous size of the army, numerous as the sands on the sea shore. They were martyrs and feared the Most High . . .

As soon as the enemy came into the courtyard, they found some of our most pious scholars there together with our brilliant master, Isaac ben Moses. He offered his neck and his was the first head they cut off. The others sat by themselves in the courtyard, wrapped in their fringed prayer shawls. They did not try to flee into the house to save their lives, but in love, they accepted God's sentence. The enemy hurled stones and arrows upon them, but they did not want to flee and 'with the sword slaughtering them and destroying them' [Esther 9: 5], the enemy murdered all of those that they found there. (Solomon bar Samson, *History*)

Extraordinary accusations were levelled against the Jews:

This we have heard from the mouth of Theobald who was himself once a Jew, but later became a monk. He told us that in the ancient writings of his ancestors, it was written that Jews could not obtain their freedom or return to their homeland without shedding human blood. It was laid down by them in the olden times that each year they must sacrifice a Christian in some part of the world to God Most High to show their contempt of Christ and so they might avenge their sufferings on him, since it was because of Christ's death that they were exiled from their own country and had to live as slaves in a strange land. (Thomas of Monmouth, *The Life and Miracles of St William of Norwich*)

Punitive measures were introduced against the Jews:

As the villainy of the Jews in the exaction of interest increases, the more the religion of Christians is restrained and the Jews quickly use up the wealth of the Christians. In order to help Christians in this matter so that they are not excessively oppressed by the Jews, we decree that if heavy and unreasonable interest is extorted, whatever the excuse, the Christians shall no more associate with them until the Jews give proper satisfaction for their unceasing oppression.

Since it would be altogether ridiculous that one who has blasphemed against Christ should hold any authority over Christians, because of the boldness of sinners, we reaffirm what the Council of Toledo has sensibly decreed. We forbid the Jews to be holders of public offices since by some excuse or other they show as much enmity towards Christians as possible. (Decrees of the Fourth Lateran Council)

Increasingly Christian kings saw the expulsion of Jews from their territories as the solution to their political and economic problems:

In the year of the incarnation of our Lord 1182, in April, which the Jews call Nisan, the most serene King Philip Augustus issued an edict that all Jews in his lands must leave by the coming feast of St John the Baptist. The king allowed them to sell all moveable goods before the festival, but their real estate such as houses, fields, vineyards, barns, winepresses and so on he kept for himself and his successors, the kings of France. (Rigord, *The Acts of Philip Augustus*)

When the Black Death raged through Europe in the fourteenth century, the Jews were accused of sorcery and murder:

Agimet the Jew took his packet of poison with him to Venice. When he arrived he scattered some of it into the well of fresh water, which was near the German house, in order to poison the people who use the well's water. He says that this is the only well of fresh water in the city and he also says that Rabbi Peyvet promised to give him whatever he wanted for his trouble in this matter. (Jacob von Königshofen, *Chronicle*)

Formal disputations between Jewish and Christian scholars were held in Paris in 1240, Barcelona in 1263 and Tortosa in 1413. The Christians were always allowed the last word:

Odo, by the grace of God, Bishop of Tusculum, Legate of the Apostolic Throne, to all whom these presents reach, greetings. You should know that . . . we examined certain Jewish books called Talmud and, before Jewish scholars and other witnesses, we pronounced the following judgment:

We found these books full of innumerable errors, blasphemies, wickednesses and abuses, most shameful to those who speak of them and most shocking to the listener. The books are so appalling that they cannot be tolerated in God's name without harming the Christian faith . . . Therefore we pronounce these books unworthy of tolerance. They may not be returned to the Jewish scholars, and we unequivocally condemn them. (Bishop Odo, *Condemnation of the Talmud*)

Initially the Jewish community of Spain had enjoyed a measure of security (see Chapter 6, Part 4), but in 1480 King Ferdinand and Queen Isabella brought the Inquisition to Spain and in 1492 the entire community was expelled:

In the year 5252 [1492], in the reign of King Ferdinand, the Lord afflicted the remnant of his people a second time and sent them into exile. The city of Granada had been captured by the king from the Moors and it had surrendered to him on 7th January. Then the King ordered the Jews to be expelled from the whole kingdom – from Castile, Catalonia, Aragon, Galicia, Majorca, Minorca, the Basque Provinces, the islands of Sardinia and Sicily and from the kingdom of Valencia. The Queen had already expelled them from Andalucia. The King granted them three months in which to leave . . . There is no agreement as to their actual numbers, but after many inquiries, I found the most usual estimate to be 50,000 families, although others maintain 53,000 families. (A contemporary Italian account of the expulsion)

Suggested Further Reading

The Koran, Harmondsworth: Penguin Books, 1968.

J. HaCohen, *The Vale of Tears*, trans. H. S. May, The Hague: Martinus Nijhoff, 1971.

L. Nemoy, ed., *A Karaite Anthology*, New Haven, CT: Yale University Press, 1952.

Rashi, *Commentary on the Pentateuch*, trans. M. Rosenbaum and A. M. Silbermann, London: Shapiro Vallentine, 1926–34.

Chronological Table

Circa CE	Documents	Events in Jewish History
100–0	Damascus Document	
0–100	The New Testament	
100–200	Tacitus' *Histories*	
200–300	Midrash	
300–400	Jerusalem Talmud; Chrysostom's *Against the Jews*	Christianity becomes the official religion of the Roman Empire
400–500	Theodosian Canon	
500–600	Babylonian Talmud	
600–700	Qur'án	Era of the Academies Rise of Islam
700–800		Rise of Karaism Era of the Exilarch and the Gaonim
800–900	Hadith	Conversion of the Khazars to Judaism. Era of Karaite biblical Scholarship
900–1000	Saadiah's *Refutation of Anan*; ben Mazliah's *Open Rebuke*; al-Kirkisani's *Book of Lights*; al-Masudi's *Library*; ibn Shaprut's letter	The Golden Age of Spain
1000–1100	ibn Gabirol's *Royal Crown*; ben Ezra's *Poems*; Rashi's *Commentary*	The Golden Age of Spain First Crusade
1100–1200	Benjamin's *Voyages*; Maimonides' *Mishneh Torah*; Thomas of Monmouth's *William of Norwich*; ibn David's *Line of Tradition*; Halevi's *Poems*; bar Samson's *History*	Almohads take control of Muslim Spain; First example of blood libel
1200–1300	Code of Alfonso X; Adret's *Responsa*; Odo's *Condemnation*; Decrees of Fourth Lateran Council, Rigord's *Acts*	Expulsion of Jews from England Christian/Jewish disputations
1300–1400	von Königshofen's *Chronicle*	Era of the Black Death
1400–1500	Italian account of expulsion	Expulsion of Jews from Spain

7

The Jewish Philosophical Tradition

1. Rabbinic Theology

The rabbis of the talmudic period were not speculative philosophers, but it is possible to reconstruct their ideas on the nature of God:

> God said to Israel: Because you have seen so many manifestations of me, this does not mean that there are many gods. It is always the same God: I am the Lord your God. R. Levi said: God appeared to them like a glass in which many faces are reflected; a thousand people look at it and it looks at each of them. Thus when God spoke to the Children of Israel, each one of them thought that he spoke personally to them. So it says: I am the Lord your [singular] God, not collectively, I am the Lord your [plural] God. (Midrash, Pes. K. 109)

> A king usually has dukes and regents who share the burdens of his office and also share in the deference he receives, but this is not so with God. God has no duke nor governor nor lieutenant. He shares his work with no one; he does it all by himself. No one else shares the burdens with him; he bears them by himself. Therefore he alone is to be worshipped. (Midrash, Psalm 149)

> R. Joshua b. Karha was asked by a pagan: Why did God speak to Moses from a thorn bush? R. Joshua replied . . . God spoke to him from a thorn bush to teach you that there is no place that the Divine Presence does not penetrate; he is even in a thorn bush. (Midrash, Exodus R.)

On God's transcendence and immanence:

> God is far off since he is in the deepest heavens, but he is also near . . . When a man goes into a synagogue and stands behind a column and prays in a whisper, God still hears his prayer. It is the same with all his creatures. Can there be a closer God than this? He is as close to his creatures as the ear is to the mouth. (Jerusalem Talmud, Berakoth IX)

R. Judah b. Simon said: An idol is near and far, but God is far and near. This is because an idol worshipper makes an idol and puts it in his house. Thus the idol is near, but however much he cries to the idol, it will not answer – and therefore it is far. But God is far and near. This is because the journey from here to Heaven takes five hundred years, and so God is far. But if a man prays and meditates in his heart, then God answers prayer and is near. (Midrash, Deuteronomy R.)

On God's justice and mercy:

If God is merciful to those who sin against his will, how much more merciful will he be to those who do his will. (Midrash, Sifre Num.)

In the hour when the Children of Israel take up their trumpets and blow them before God, God rises up from the throne of his judgement and sits down upon the throne of his mercy. He is filled with compassion for his people and the attribute of justice is turned into the attribute of mercy. (Midrash, Sifre Num.)

On the pre-existence of the Torah:

Through the Torah God created the world, the Torah was his helper and his tool. With its aid he set boundaries to the deep, ordered the orbits of the sun and the moon and formed all of nature. Without the Torah, the world would disappear. (Midrash, Tanh. B.)

On God's omniscience and human free will:

Before man's heart can even conjecture a thought, God knows it already. Even before a human being is created, his thought is known to God. (Midrash, Genesis R.)

All who of their own free will draw near to God, God draws near to them. (Midrash, Sifre Num.)

On the selection of Israel and the status of other nations:

All the nations of the world were invited to receive the Torah . . . They were asked, but they did not accept it . . . But when he came to Israel, they all declared: All that the Lord has commanded, we will do, and we will be obedient [Exodus 24: 7]. Again since the Children of Noah cannot keep the Seven Commandments, how much less could they have accepted the whole of the Torah? (Midrash, Mekhilta Bahodesh)

On human destiny and the afterlife:

R. Johanan said: The prophets only prophesied for the days of the messiah; but no eye has seen what God has prepared for those who serve him in the World to Come. (Talmud, Berakoth XXXIV)

God said to Moses: Behold your days draw near to die. [Deuteronomy 31: 14]. Samuel bar Nahmani said: Do days die? It means that when the righteous die, their days end in the world, but they stay, as it is written: In whose hand is the soul of all the living [Job 12: 10]. Does this mean that the living, but not the dead are in the hands of God? No. It means that even after death, the righteous are still living, but the wicked, both when they are alive and when they are dead, may be described as dead. (Midrash, Tanh. B.)

On the human soul:

It is written: Praise the Lord O my soul [Psalms 103: 1]. Why did David praise God with his soul? He said: The soul fills the body and God fills the world [Jeremiah 23: 24] . . . The soul supports the body and God supports the world [Isaiah 46: 4] . . . The soul outlives the body and God outlives the world [Psalms 102: 27] . . . The soul is all by itself in the body and God is all by himself in the world [Deuteronomy 6: 4] . . . The soul does not eat in the body and God does not eat [Psalms 50: 13] . . . The soul sees, but is invisible; God sees, but is invisible [Zechariah 4: 10] . . . The soul is pure in the body and God is pure in the world [Habakkuk 1: 13] . . . The soul does not sleep in the body just like God, who also does not sleep. (Midrash, Leviticus R.)

2. Philo and Saadiah Gaon

In the first century CE, the Alexandrian philosopher, Philo, had tried to integrate Greek philosophy and Jewish teaching into a unified whole by explaining the God of Judaism in Greek philosophical terms:

Some people insist that the non-physical Forms are an empty concept reflecting nothing in reality. In saying this they deny the essential nature of existing things, namely the archetypes of all the qualities of being according to which everything is given form and size. The Holy Tablets of the Law speak of these as 'crushed'; in the same way as anything which is crushed has lost its shape and nature and is, so to speak, undifferentiated matter, similarly the doctrine that denies the existence of the Forms confuses everything and reduces it to a shapeless mass. What could be more absurd? God created everything from primordial matter although he did not touch it himself because it is not lawful for the glorious Blessed One to touch chaotic, limitless matter. Instead he used his spiritual powers, which should be called

Forms, to give each species its distinctive shape. To suggest otherwise leads to confusion and disorder. By denying the Forms which produced the particular qualities, a man denies the existence of the qualities themselves. (Philo, *On the Special Laws*)

Nine hundred years later, Saadiah Gaon was attempting to confront the challenges of the Karaites (see Chapter 6, Part 3), the Muslim theologians (see Chapter 6, Part 2), the Zoroastrians (who were attacking the whole concept of monotheism) and the Hellenistic philosophers (who saw no need for a divine creator at all):

I should like to explain why people have doubts, deny miracles and lose their faith in God. I would suggest that the eight most common causes are as follows: firstly, people are usually reluctant to think deeply about matters. Therefore when they meet something that might strengthen their faith in the Torah, they are frightened and run away from it. Because of this you find people saying that truth is hard, or that truth is bitter. They do not want to be involved in the whole business and so they run away . . .

Secondly is the fact that many people are stupid and talk foolishly and seem bent on idleness. So whenever they meet a valuable idea, they satisfy their inner conscience by insisting that there is nothing in it.

The third cause of religious doubt is that man is determined to satisfy his desire for food, drink, possessions and sexual satisfaction. He is so preoccupied with these things that he gives no thought to anything else . . .

The fourth cause of religious doubt is that people are indifferent and unreflective when they come across a true idea. They just say to themselves: I have thought all about that, but it does not mean anything to me . . .

The fifth cause of religious doubt is human pride and contempt. Once these vices take possession of a man, they stop him from admitting his ignorance on any matter of philosophy – indeed often he cannot even perceive the issue . . .

The sixth cause of religious doubt is the result of hearing the words of an unbeliever. These touch his heart and damage it and this damage can last for the remainder of his life . . .

The seventh cause of religious doubt is the result of hearing a feeble argument in support of faith. He sees that the argument is nonsense and therefore he thinks all the arguments of believers should be ridiculed . . .

The eighth cause of religious doubt is the result of personal hatred of individual believers. This hatred can lead to a hatred of the God in whom they believe . . .

It is also possible that people hold false beliefs because they find verses in the scripture which seem to be untrue; or they pray to God and their prayer is not answered; or they ask God for something and they do not receive it; or they see that God does not always punish the wicked; or they notice unbelievers holding high office; or they see that death destroys human beings indiscriminately; or they cannot grasp the notion of God's unity or the idea of the soul or the belief in reward and punishment. I shall discuss all these topics at the proper time and place and will do my best to explain them. I hope that with God's aid, I will be able to help those who share the journey with me. (Saadiah Gaon, *The Book of Beliefs and Opinions*)

Saadiah was influenced by the Muslim Kalam philosophers who had argued that truth could be discerned through the experience of the senses, through the intuition of self-evident truths, through logical reasoning and through reliable tradition:

We must immediately accept the teachings of religion, together with all its implications, because they are confirmed by the evidence of our senses. They have also been handed down by reliable tradition which will be discussed later. However, we are also commanded by God to take time in making rational inquiries and arrive at the truth of religion by logical argument. We must not abandon our attempts until we have found convincing arguments and are forced to believe the revelation of God from the evidence of our own eyes and ears. Sometimes these inquiries take a long time, but we should not worry about that . . . We can compare the quest to the case of someone who immediately identifies his own illness from its key characteristic symptoms and that diagnosis is subsequently confirmed after a thorough and complete investigation. (Ibid.)

3. The Jewish Philosophers of Mediaeval Spain

The earliest Spanish philosopher to produce work in the Neoplatonic tradition was Solomon ben Joseph ibn Gabirol, writing in the eleventh century:

Pupil: Is the essence of universal being single or multiple?
Master: It is definitely multiple. But even though it is diverse and multiple, it resolves into two principles, in which two it is sustained and has being.
Pupil: What are these two?
Master: Universal matter and universal form.
Pupil: But how can the totality of all that exists be resolved into these two principles?
Master: Because these two are at the root of everything and from them is generated everything that exists . . .
The Universal soul sustains the entire corporeal world and imagines whatever is in it and sees it. In the same way, our own individual soul sustains our body and imagines and sees whatever is in it. (Solomon ibn Gabirol, *The Fountain of Life*)

Another philosopher of the golden age of Spanish Jewry was Bahya ben Joseph ibn Pakuda, the author of an immensely popular ethical guide known as *The Duties of the Heart*. This also was influenced by Neoplatonism:

> The first duty of man is to study the origin of the human being, his birth, the construction of the different parts of his physical body, the joining together of each of his limbs, the use of each of the limbs and the reasons why he must be so constructed. Then man's advantages must be studied, his different moods, his soul's faculties, the light of his intellect, his essential and accidental qualities, his desires and the reasons for his existence. When we have grasped all these matters with regard to human beings, many of the mysteries of the universe will be revealed since man resembles the universe. For this reason some wise men define philosophy as man's knowledge of man. By understanding the nature of the human being, he will see evidence of God's wisdom revealed in himself and he will thus know his Creator. As Job put it, 'From my flesh, I see God' [Job 19: 26]. (Bahya ibn Pakuda, *Duties of the Heart*)

Another important philosopher of this golden age of Spanish Jewry was Abraham ibn Daud who was influenced by Aristotelianism and was writing in the twelfth century:

> We notice that the elements move in different directions. Fire and air tend to move upwards while earth and air tend to move downwards. If the elements move in their particular direction by virtue of their corporeality, then they would all move in one direction – a direction would be common to all of them in the same way as corporeality is common to all of them. Similarly if they all move by virtue of their matter, then they would all move in one direction – since matter . . . is common to all of them. These elements could not be moved in different directions by corporeality or by matter – so it follows that the cause of the motion of a body is not the body itself. This is an important principle. Keep it in mind. (Abraham ibn Daud, *Exalted Faith*)

Perhaps the best known Jewish thinker of the era was Judah Halevy. In his *Kuzari*, he defended the doctrines of Judaism against the teachings of Christianity, Islam and Aristotelianism:

> The philosophers of ancient times are justified in their use of rational argument because they did not have the benefit either of the words of the prophets or the light of revelation. In any science which depends on proof, they attained the highest degree of perfection and indeed studied such sciences with the greatest possible concentration. And they all agree about their findings. Yet they did not achieve similar unanimity in other, later sciences

– such as metaphysics or even physics. If a group of them did reach agreement on a particular issue, this is not because they had all carried out an
individual empirical study and had all come to the same conclusion.
Rather it was because they were all disciples of a single school of philosophy and they all blindly affirmed the views of the founder of that
school. (Examples of such schools include that of Pythagoras,
Empedocles, Aristotle or Plato. Alternatively they might be Companions
of the Porch or a member of the Perapatetics who follow the ideas of
Aristotle . . .) Their intentions were good. They did state the laws of rational thought and they did turn away from the vanities of the world.
Certainly they are not compelled to accept our opinion and, in that sense,
they may be considered superior. Nonetheless, as far as we are concerned,
we must accept whatever our eyes show us and we also accept any well-
attested tradition – which is the same thing as seeing for ourselves. (Judah
Halevy, *The Kuzari*)

4. Moses Maimonides and the Maimonidean Controversy

Rabbi Moses ben Maimon (1135–1204), known as Maimonides or
Rambam, made a major contribution to both the legal and the philosophical tradition. His *Mishneh Torah* (Second Law) was intended as a code,
a synthesis of Jewish law:

A man should not be jokey or frivolous; nor should he be sad and gloomy;
he should be calm. Our wise men declare: Jokes and frivolity lead a man to
lewdness. They say that a man should not laugh or grieve or mourn too easily, but should meet everyone with a cheerful expression. Also a man should
not be over-ambitious or too eager to do well; nor should he be too pess-
imistic so that he never accomplishes anything. But he should be open-hand-
ed; he should do a little business; he should study the Law and he should be
grateful for whatever he has. He should not be quick to quarrel, or envy the
good fortune of others, or be lecherous or anxious for fame. The wise men
say: Jealousy, ambition and lust put a man out of this world. In other words,
a man should work towards the mean of each characteristic so that all his
character traits are directed towards the middle path. That is what Solomon
means when he says: Take heed to the path of your feet, then all your ways
will be sure. Do not swerve to the right or to the left. (Proverbs 4: 26–7)
(Maimonides, *Mishneh Torah*)

His *Guide of the Perplexed* was an attempt to reconcile the contradictions
between fashionable Aristotelian philosophy with the traditional teachings of the rabbis:

You should know that God (may he be exalted and praised!) can only correctly be described by negative attributes. A negative description is not tainted by fanciful exaggeration and does not imply that God is deficient in any general or particular way. On the other hand, if God is described by positive attributes, as we have made clear, this implies that he is connected with things other than himself and this indicates a deficiency in him. First I will make it clear how negations are, in some sense, attributes and how they differ from affirmative attributes. Then I will show that we are not able to describe him in any way except by describing what he is not. (Maimonides, *The Guide of the Perplexed* I)

The opinion of all those who believe in the Law of Moses our Master (peace be on him!) is that the whole universe, by which I mean everything that is in existence except for God (may he be exalted!), came into being through God. Before its creation, it was purely and totally non-existent and God, (May He be exalted!) existed by himself with nothing else – not with an angel, not with a sphere, not with what is within a sphere. Then, entirely through his own will, he brought everything into existence, as it is now, out of nothing. Even time is one of his created things since time depends on motion, and motion is an accident of whatever is moved. Also whatever is moved . . . was itself created in time. It came into existence after it had been nothing. Therefore when we say: God was in existence before he created the world – the word 'was' indicates that it occurred in time – and in fact all the ideas we have about the infinite duration of God 'before' the creation of the universe – all depend on a human conception or imagining of time, not on what is really the case. Time is unquestionably an accident. We maintain that it is a created accident like blackness or whiteness. Although it is not, like blackness or whiteness, a quality, it is nonetheless an accident depending on motion, as anyone who has understood Aristotle's discourse explaining time and the true nature of existence will appreciate. (Ibid., II)

I maintain that food forbidden in the Law is not wholesome . . . The main reason why the Law forbids the flesh of pigs is because of the fact that a pig's food and habits are very disgusting and dirty. It has already been shown how the Law unequivocally commands the removal of horrible objects from sight even from the field or the camp. Such sights are even more offensive in the town. If eating the flesh of pigs is allowed, streets and houses would be filthier than any cesspit – as one can see in present day France. Our wise men used to say: The mouth of a pig is as dirty as manure . . . All the commandments about the killing of animals are necessary. As every doctor knows very well, meat is a natural food for human beings. Therefore the Law commands us that animals should be killed as mercifully as possible. It is wrong to torture a creature by cutting its throat clumsily or by poleaxing it, or by cutting off its limbs while it is still alive. (Ibid.)

Maimonides' philosophy was the focus for a series of controversies during his lifetime and after. The philosopher Nachmanides argued that Maimonides' philosophy was essential if the assimilated upper-class Jews of Spain and Provence were to be kept within the Jewish fold:

> Their bellies are full of the folly of the Greeks . . . They make mock of souls who are trusting . . . they do not deeply follow the Law and they are content to imitate the ways of foreign children. If it were not for his [Maimonides'] words . . . they would have lapsed almost completely. (Nachmanides, letter to the French rabbis)

Rabbi Solomon ibn Adret even issued a ban against those who studied philosophy before the age of twenty-five:

> Therefore we have decreed for ourselves, our children and for all those that join us, that for the next fifty years and under threat of being banned from the community, no one among us under the age of twenty-five shall study either in the original or in translation books written by the Greeks on religious philosophy or natural science . . . Excluded, however, from this general ban are books on the science of medicine. Although medicine is a natural science, the Law allows a doctor to heal. (Solomon ibn Adret, *Ban*)

5. Later Jewish Philosophy

The most prominent Jewish scholar after Maimonides was Levi ben Gershom, known as Gersonides (1288–1344) who, like Maimonides, was attracted to Aristotelianism:

> Now that we have shown that the object of knowledge is not a Universal, but either an individual concept or an individual proposition, it is clear that the claim that the objects of knowledge are universal is a false claim. We have also demonstrated that the universality which is, in some sense, inherent in the universal proposition does not imply that the object of knowledge is different from what actually exists in reality. In fact, that is the opposite of what our argument is trying to show. Knowledge is acquired from repeated exposure to individual examples, when the intellect abstracts from the individual its material accidents. From these material accidents plurality accrues to the individual. (Gersonides, *The Wars of the Lord* I)

The last major philosopher of Spanish Jewry was Hasdai Crescas (1340–1412). He distanced himself from the philosophy of Maimonides:

> Therefore, following this plan, it seems correct to divide Book I into three parts. The first will be a commentary in which [Maimonides'] propositions

are proved, using the arguments which the philosophers themselves use in their own writings. It will also restate the Master's [Maimonides'] proofs [for God's existence]. Since we will critically examine both the propositions and the proofs, so we must make every attempt to explain them and thoroughly clarify them just as the Master himself would have wanted them to be explained. The second part will be an examination of both proofs and propositions to see whether they have been demonstrated conclusively. The third part will be a discussion of the same principles, interpreted in accordance with the strict teachings of the Bible. We will also explain how we reached these principles. Thus the purpose of Book I will be revealed – namely that we cannot fully grasp these principles except in the light of prophecy, as far as the words of prophecy are borne witness to in the scriptures and are indirectly confirmed in our tradition. It will also be shown that these teaching do not necessarily contradict the findings of reason. (Hasdai Crescas, *The Light of the Lord*)

After Crescas, Jewish philosophers became more concerned with defining the essential doctrines of Judaism. Maimonides had already outlined his thirteen principles of the Jewish faith:

The fundamental principles of our Law are thirteen in number:
The first fundamental principle is the existence of the Creator . . .
The second principle is the Oneness of God . . .
The third principle is the denial that God has a body . . .
The fourth principle is God's pre-existence . . .
The fifth principle is that God is the one who should be magnified and worshipped . . .
The sixth principle is prophecy . . .
The seventh principle is the prophecy of Moses, our teacher. We should believe that Moses is the father of the prophets . . .
The eighth principle is that our Law is from Heaven . . .
The ninth principle is not being taken away. The Law of Moses will not be taken away . . .
The tenth principle is that God knows the deeds of human beings . . .
The eleventh principle is that God rewards those who keep the commandments of the Law and punishes those who break them . . .
The twelfth principle concerns the messianic age. We believe and affirm that the Messiah will come . . .
The thirteenth principle is the resurrection of the dead.
(Maimonides, *Commentary on the Mishnah*)

Joseph Albo was critical of Maimonides' principles:

A man may keep the Law of Moses and believe in its principles. Yet when he looks more deeply into the matter, examining the texts and using his reason, he may be deceived in his conjectures and he may interpret a principle differently from its apparent meaning; alternatively he may deny a principle because he does not think it supports what our Law tells us we must believe; or again he may mistakenly insist that something is not a fundamental principle even though he accepts it as he accepts other non-fundamental elements in our Law; perhaps he calls into question one of the miracles and he does not see that in denying it, he is denying a fundamental doctrine which he must believe on the authority of our Law. A man of this sort is not an unbeliever. Rather he must be numbered with the wise and pious men of Israel, even though his ideas are mistaken. (Joseph Albo, *Book of Principles*)

In the same vein, Isaac Abravanel insisted that true religion depended on divine revelation and could not be discerned by philosophical speculation:

I have set out Maimonides' teaching on prophecy and I must now examine whether that teaching is true and whether it accords with the fundamental principle of our Law. I have to say that Maimonides conjectured 'with the line of confusion' and 'the plummet of chaos' [Isaiah 34: 11] when he declared that prophecy is a natural phenomenon that comes to suitably qualified people in the same way as natural forms come to the substrata. This is false. Prophecy comes from God like other miracles. It is not a natural happening, but a miraculous event. We can prove its miraculous nature by pointing out that prophecy is only found among the Israelite people, and only among them when they serve the most glorious God in his Promised Land. It never occurs under other conditions. Therefore prophecy cannot be a natural phenomenon because it is not found among all the nations and every country at every date. (Isaac Abravanel, *Commentary on Prophecy*)

By the end of the fifteenth century succeeding generations had turned away from philosophy and preferred mystical speculation for the explanation of ultimate questions.

Suggested Further Reading

S. Gaon, *Book of Beliefs and Opinions*, trans. S. Rosenblatt, New Haven, CT: Yale University Press, 1948.

I. Husik, *A History of Medieval Jewish Philosophy*, Philadelphia: Jewish Publication Society, 1958.

Y. Halevi, *Book of the Kuzari*, Brooklyn, NY: P. Shalom, n.d.

M. Maimonides, *The Guide of the Perplexed*, Chicago: Chicago University Press, 1974.

Chronological Table

Circa CE	Documents
0–100	Philo's *Special Laws*
200–300	Midrash
300–400	Jerusalem Talmud
500–600	Babylonian Talmud
800–900	Saadiah's *Beliefs and Opinions*
1000–1100	ibn Gabirol's *Fountain of Life*
1100–1200	Bahya's *Duties*; Halevy's *Kuzari*; ibn Daud's *Exalted Faith*; Maimonides' *Guide*, *Second Law* and *Commentary*
1200–1300	Nachmanides' letter; ibn Adret's *Ban*
1300–1400	Crescas' *Light*
1400–1500	Albo's *Principles*; Abravanel's *Commentary*

8

Mysticism

1. Early Rabbinic Mysticism

One of the most important texts of mystical speculation dates from as early as the second century CE and is known as the *Sefer Yetzirah* ('The Book of Creation'). According to this, God created the universe through a process of emanation:

> There are ten intangible emanations . . . ten and not nine, ten and not eleven. Understand with wisdom and be wise with understanding, test them and explore them . . . Understand the matter completely and set the Creator in his place . . . He alone is the Creator and Former. There is no one else. His attributes are ten and infinite . . . There are ten intangible emanations, whose end is fixed in their beginning, just as a flame is bound to a coal . . .
>
> One: Spirit of the Living God, blessed and blest is the name of him who lives forever . . . His beginning has no beginning, his end has no end . . .
>
> Two: Spiritual Air from Spirit. He engraved land and hewed out in it twenty-two letters as a foundation . . .
>
> Three: Spiritual Water from Spiritual Air; he engraved and hewed out in it chaos and disorder, mud and mire . . .
>
> Four: Spiritual Fire from Spiritual Water; he engraved and hewed out in it the throne of glory, Seraphim . . . and Ministering Angels . . .
>
> Five: He sealed Height . . .
>
> Six: He sealed Depth . . .
>
> Seven: He sealed East . . .
>
> Eight: He sealed West . . .
>
> Nine: He sealed South . . .
>
> Ten: He sealed North . . .
>
> These intangible emanations are One . . . Spirit of the Living God, Spiritual Air from Spirit, Spiritual Water from Spiritual Air, Spiritual Fire from Spiritual Water, Height, Depth, East, West, South and North.

In addition to the ten emanations, the *Book of Creation* depicts the process of Creation as taking place through the twenty-two Hebrew letters:

By means of the twenty-two letters, by giving them a form and shape, by mixing them and combining them in different ways, God made the soul of all that has been created and all that will be . . . The three mother letters, aleph, mem and shin are in the universe: air, water and fire . . . He caused the letter Bet to reign over life . . . He caused the letter Gimel to reign over peace . . . He caused the letter Dalet to reign over wisdom . . . He caused the letter Kaf to reign over wealth . . . He caused the letter Pey to reign over gracefulness . . . He caused the letter Resh to reign over seed . . . He caused the letter Tav to reign over dominion . . . The twelve simple letters: Hey, Vav, Zayin, Chet, Tet, Yod, Lamed, Nun, Samek, Ayin, Tzade, Kof. Their foundations of sight, hearing, smell, speech, tasting, sexual congress, work, movement, anger, laughter, thought and sleep. Twelve constellations in the universe. Twelve months in the year. Twelve organs in the body of male and female.

Another early mystical tradition found in the midrash and Talmud is connected with Ezekiel's vision of the chariot (Ezekiel 1: 28). It was the aim of the mystic to free himself from the chains of bodily existence and become a 'chariot rider', although the whole enterprise was fraught with danger:

R. Johanan ben Zakkai was once riding on a donkey and R. Eleazar ben Arach was on a donkey behind him. R. Eleazar ben Arach said to R. Johanan ben Zakkai: O master, teach me a chapter of the chariot mysteries. . . . The master replied: No! Have I not already informed you that the chariot may not be taught to any one man by himself unless he is a sage and of an original turn of mind? Eleazar ben Arach replied: Very well then. Will you give me your permission to tell you something you taught me? Johanan ben Zakkai replied: Yes! Say it! . . . Then Eleazar ben Arach began his discourse on the mysteries of the chariot and, no sooner had he begun, than fire came down from Heaven and encompassed all the trees of the field, which with one accord burst into song . . . Upon this, an angel cried out from the fire, saying: Truly these, even these, are the secrets of the chariot. (Talmud, Haggigah 14)

The Riders of the Chariot were making the ascent to the heavenly halls:

The horses are horses of darkness, horses of shadow, horses of gloom, horses of fire, horses of blood, horses of hail, horses of iron, horses of cloud . . . This is a description of the guardians at the door of the seventh hall and the horses at the door of each hall. All the masters would descend into the chariot and would also ascend again and not be harmed, even though they saw everything in the heavenly hall. They would descend in peace and return, and would stand and bear witness to the fearsome, confounding visions of things not found in the place of any mortal king. Then they would bless, praise, sing out . . . and give glory . . . to the Lord God of Israel, who rejoices in those who descend in the chariot. (Midrash, *The Greater Heavenly Halls*)

All these mystical speculations were shrouded in secrecy:

The name of the forty-two letters can only be entrusted to a person who is modest and meek, in the midway of life, not easily provoked to anger, temperate and free from vengeful feelings. He who understands it, is cautious with it and keeps it in purity, is loved above and liked here below. He is revered by his fellow men, he is heir to two worlds – this world and the world to come. (Talmud, Haggigah 13)

2. The Hasidei Ashkenaz

Against the background of the Crusades and increasing anti-Semitism in Western Europe, the Hasidei Ashkenaz (the Pious Men of Germany) explored the Jewish mystical tradition to help their fellow Jews face the trial of Christian persecution:

It is forbidden to accustom oneself to flattery. A man must beware of saying what he does not mean, and instead must say whatever is in his heart – his speech should reflect his beliefs. A man must not deceive anyone, and that includes a non-Jew . . . A man must not press another to eat when he knows he will not do so, nor give presents to someone when he knows they will not be accepted. A man may not open a bottle of wine, suggesting he is doing so in honour of someone, when in fact the barrel has to be opened in any case . . . The same applies to all similar situations – even a word of deception is forbidden. One must be truthful in speech, upright in spirit and one's heart should be free of all perversity and vanity. (Judah HeHasid, *Book of the Pious*)

There is a kind of piety that is pernicious. For example, when a man whose hands are ritually unclean sees a holy book fall into the fire and says that it is better that the book is burned than that it is touched with unclean hands. Another example might be when a man sees a woman drowning in the river and says that it is better that the woman drown than that he touch her when she is ritually unclean. (Ibid.)

The root of saintliness is for a man to go beyond the letter of the Law, as it is written: And gracious in all his works. (Psalms 145: 17)

The root of fear is when it is hard for a man to do the thing, as it is written: For now I know that thou art a God-fearing man. (Genesis 22: 12)

The root of prayer is that the heart rejoices in the love of the holy one, blessed be he, as it is written: Let the heart of them rejoice that seek the Lord. (I Chronicles 16: 10) which is why David used to play on the harp.

The root of our Law is to study with profundity so as to know how to carry out all God's commands, as it is written: A good understanding in all they do. (Psalms 111: 10)

The root of the fear of the Lord is when a man desires something and yet he gives up the pleasure for which his evil inclination craves because he fears the Lord . . .

The root of love is to love the Lord. The soul is full of love, bound with the bounds of love in great joy. The joy chases away from his heart all bodily pleasures and worldly delights . . .

The root of humility is that man keeps himself far from the honour paid to noblemen . . .

Carry out all your good deeds in secret and walk humbly with your God . . .

In all places and especially in the synagogue where the Divine Presence is in front of you, sit in his presence in dread and set your heart to give thanks unto him . . .

The soul is filled with love, bound with the bonds of love in great joy. This joy chases away all bodily pleasure and worldly delight from his heart. The powerful joy of love seizes his heart so that he continually thinks: How can I do God's will? The pleasures of his children and the company of his wife are as nothing in comparison with the love of God. Imagine a young man who has not been with a woman for a long time. He longs for her; his heart burns for her. Imagine his great love and desire when he cohabits with her and how he has so much pleasure when his sperm shoots like an arrow. All this is nothing compared with his desire to do God's will, to bring merit to others, to sanctify himself, to sacrifice his life in love. (Eleazar ben Judah, *Secret of Secrets*)

According to the Hasidei Ashkenaz, prayer was a process of mystical ascent. The following prayer, the Hymn of Glory composed at this time, gained a central place in the liturgy:

He loves his people, his humble seed he glorifies,
He who is surrounded by men's praise, takes delight in them.
O you who have called into being the generations,
Extend your care to a people who yearn for you.

Receive the multitude of my hymns,
And may the song of my prayer come before you.
Let my prayer be like incense,
Let a poor man's song be to you
As the song once chanted at the altar of sacrifice.
May my prayer come before you,
The Creator and Sustainer of the Universe,
The just and mighty one.
Accept the silent promptings of my heart,
For my whole being is astir with longing for your presence.

3. The Emergence of the Zohar

At the same time mystical works were being produced in southern France.
In the *Book of Bahir*, the ten sefirot (emanations) of God are structured as
a cosmic tree:

> What is this tree of which you speak? He said to him: It refers to the powers
> of God [the sefirot] in graded order and they are like a tree. As a tree by being
> watered bears fruit, so the Holy One, by means of water, increases the powers
> of the tree. And what is the water of the Holy One, blessed be he? It is wis-
> dom. And this also refers to the souls of the righteous that are carried from the
> spring to the great channel and ascend and are attached to the tree. And through
> what are they carried? Through the people of Israel: when they are righteous
> and virtuous, the Divine Presence lives among them and their words are in the
> lap of the Holy One, blessed be he, and he causes them to prosper and increase.

The *Book of Bahir* also taught a doctrine of the transmigration of souls:

> Why is it that there is a righteous person who enjoys good and there is a
> righteous person who suffers? It is because in the latter case the righteous
> person was formerly wicked and for this reason he is punished. But is one
> punished for offences committed during one's youth? . . . I do not refer to
> misdeeds in the course of a person's life. I refer to the fact that a person pre-
> existed prior to his present life.

Rabbi Azriel ben Menahem of Gerona, writing in the early thirteenth
century, drew on Neoplatonic ideas in his *Gate of Intent*:

> Imagine that you yourself are light and that all of your surroundings on every
> side are also light . . . There is a light called Brilliance and to its left you will
> find a light called Radiance. Directly between them is a light called Glory.
> Around it is a light called Life. Above it is the Crown. This is the light that
> crowns the desires of the mind and illuminates the paths of the imagination.

. . . From this light comes desire, blessing, peace, life and all good to those who keep the way of its unification . . . The true path is straight, depending on the concentration of the individual. He must know how to concentrate on its truth . . . According to the strength of his concentration, he will transmit power through his desire, desire through his knowledge, imagination through his thoughts, strength through his effort and fortitude through his contemplation. When there is no other thought or desire intermingled it can become so strong that it can transmit an influence from the Infinite. . . . An individual can thus ascend through the power of concentration from one thing to the next until he reaches the Infinite.

Influenced by the Hasidei Ashkenaz and the Sufi traditions of Islam, Abraham ben Samuel Abulafia (1240–71) explained how the Hebrew letters of the alphabet could be combined to fulfil the human aspiration toward prophecy:

Now begin to combine a few or many letters, to permute and to combine them until your heart is warm. Then be mindful of their movements and of what you can bring forth by moving them. When you feel your heart is already warm, and when you see that by combinations of letters you can grasp new things which by human tradition or by yourself you would not be able to know and when you are thus prepared to receive the influx of the Divine Power that flows into you, then turn all true thoughts to imagine his exalted angels in your heart as if they were human beings sitting or standing about you . . . Having imagined this very vividly, turn your whole mind to understand the many things which will come into your heart through the letters imagined. (Abraham Abulafia, *The Book of the World to Come*)

Most significant of all was the appearance of the *Zohar* at the end of the thirteenth century. Although its major part was composed by Rabbi Moses of Leon, it was set in the time of the Bar Kokhba Revolt (see Chapter 5, Part 1) and focused on Rabbi Simeon bar Yohai and his disciples:

Rabbi Eleazar asked Rabbi Simeon: We know that the Whole Offering is connected to the Holy of Holies so that it may be illumined. To what heights does the attachment of the will of the priests, the Levites and the Israelites extend? He said: We have already taught that it extends to the Infinite. For all its attachment, unification and completion is to be secreted in that secret which is neither perceived or known, and which contains the will of all wills . . .

The Infinite brings everything from potentiality to actuality; he varies his deeds, but there is no variety in him. It is he who puts the emanations in order . . . Since he is within these ten emanations, he created, designed and formed everything with them . . . It is he that binds all the chariots of the angels, and binds them together. He supports the upper and lower worlds. Were he to remove himself from them, they would have neither sustenance, knowledge or life. There is no place where he is not, above and without end, below and without limit and on every side there is no God but he.

The Zohar explains that the emanations are arranged in the form of a human body:

> You are the one who guides the emanations . . . You have prepared garments for them . . . They are named in this arrangement as follows: love – right arm; power – left arm; beauty – torso; eternity and glory – two legs; foundation – the completion of the body, the sign of the holy covenant; kingdom – the mouth, which we call the Oral Torah. The brain is intelligence, the inner thought; wisdom is the heart . . . the supernal crown is the crown of royalty.

According to the Zohar, the final goal of the mystical quest is devekut (cleaving to God):

> Happy is the portion of whoever can penetrate into the mysteries of his master and become absorbed in them. Especially does a man achieve this when he offers up his prayer to his master in intense devotion . . . Whilst his mouth and lips are moving, his heart and will must soar to the height of heights, so as to acknowledge the unity of the whole in virtue of the mystery of mysteries in which all ideas, all wills and all thoughts find their goal – that is, the mystery of the Infinite.

By the sixteenth century the doctrines of the Zohar had spread throughout Europe and Byzantium and had become an integral part of mainstream Jewish culture.

4. Lurianic Kabbalah

Joseph Caro (1488–1575), who is primarily remembered for his great legal code, the Shulhan Arukh ('Prepared Table') was also a noted mystic:

> Then slumber came upon me and I slept for about half an hour. I awoke in distress since he [Caro's heavenly mentor] did not converse with me at length as previously. I began once more to rehearse the Mishnah and before I had completed two chapters, the voice of my beloved began to knock in my mouth saying: Although you imagined I had forsaken you and left you, do not think I really will leave you before I have fulfilled my promise not to withhold good from your mouth. You must cleave to me and to the fear of

me, as I have said, and then you will be elevated, lifted up and made high before all the members of the heavenly academy, all of whom send you greetings because you busy yourself all the time with the Talmud and the codes and combine the two. (Joseph Caro, *The Heavenly Mentor*)

Caro had settled in Safed in Israel, which was a centre of mystical scholarship at this time. Among the other prominent kabbalists (students of mysticism) were Moses Cordovero (1522–70) and Isaac Luria (1534–72):

> If a man is pure and upright in deed, and if he grasps the cords of love existing in the holy roots of his soul, he will be able to ascend to every level in the whole supernal universe. When a man is upright and righteous, he can meditate with suitable thoughts and thereby ascend through the levels of the transcendental. He must unify the levels of his soul, joining one part to another, drawing the different levels of his soul to vest themselves in one another. It thereby becomes like a single candelabrum made up of different parts joined together. The individual must then unify the emanations, bringing them to bind themselves together with a strong knot. He and his soul thus become a channel through which the emanations can exert influence. (Moses Cordovero, *The Orchard of Pomegranates*)

In his study *Pleasant Light*, Cordovero offered a defence of mystical exploration:

> We have noted that there are those who keep away from this knowledge. They can be divided into three groups. Some shun it saying that there is no need to believe in a secret dimension of our Law . . . There is a second category of individuals who spurn this knowledge and their position is justified by various arguments. Although they all agree in their esteem for this knowledge, yet some argue that it is so exalted that not all are worthy to be involved in it . . . There is a third group that keep away from this knowledge by arguing that a man is prone to err in these subjects and commit sin by falling into one of those errors concerning the Divine . . . The group whose approach is acceptable consists of those who pursue the right course. They have attained some mastery in Bible and in Gemara with its teachings, which have the same status to us as the Mishnah and they have attained some mastery in this knowledge. They study it [mystical knowledge] for its own sake in order to enter into its secrets, to know their Creator, and to attain the wonderful quality of reaching the true understanding of the teaching of the Torah, of praying before the Creator, to effect unification between God and his divine presence through the performance of his commandments.

Isaac Luria in particular can be said to have transformed the mystical tradition. His teachings were recorded by his disciple Hayyim Vital:

Know that before the emanations were emanated and the creatures created, the simple supernal of light of the Infinite filled everything there was. There was no empty area at all, no empty atmosphere, no vacuum. All was filled with that simple infinite light. It had neither beginning nor end. All was simple light in total sameness . . . When in his simple will the Infinite resolved to create words and emanate the emanations, to bring to objective existence the perfection of his deeds, his names and his appellations, which was the reason for the creation of the world, he contracted in the middle point in himself, in the very centre . . . After this contraction . . . when there was left a vacuum, an empty atmosphere, through the mediation of the light of the Infinite, blessed be he, there was now available an area in which there could be the emanations, the beings created, formed and made. (Hayyim Vital, *The Tree of Life*)

Reincarnation plays an important part in Luria's system as described by another disciple:

Know that an individual may at times be perfected by temporarily joining the body of another person and at times he may require reincarnation which is even more painful. The penalty for anyone who finds a lost object but does not return it is that he will not find justification by joining after his death. Rather he will have to return it when he is reincarnated. This is the meaning of the final section of the verse: You shall not hide yourself. (Jacob Zemah, *Leader and Commander*)

In his teaching, Luria described his method of meditation:

It is very beneficial to meditate on a yichud [unification of letters] while lying prostrate on the grave of a saint. When you do so, contemplate that through your own position, you are causing the saint to prostrate his soul and infuse the bones in his grave. This, in a sense, causes him to come to life, since his bones become like a body for the soul that infuses them . . . If you are not on a grave, but meditate on yichudim at home, you need not have this intent. But at all times, whether on a grave or at home, it is helpful to imagine that your soul and the soul of the saint are bound together, with your soul included in his, and that the two of them are ascending together. (Hayyim Vital, *The Gate of the Holy Spirit*)

This mystical activity was not infrequently accompanied by supernatural manifestations:

One Sabbath morning I was preaching to the congregation in Jerusalem. Rachel, the sister of Rabbi Judah Mishan, was present. She told me that during the whole of my sermon there was a pillar of fire above my head and Elijah, of blessed memory, was there at my right hand to support me and that when I had finished they both departed. (Hayyim Vital, *Book of Visions*)

5. Shabbetai Zevi and Moses Luzzatto

Shabbetai Zevi (1626–76) was seen by many throughout the Jewish world as the Messiah. Although he seems to have had no mystical ideas of his own, he was a follower of Isaac Luria. The following contemporary account gives an idea of the excitement he inspired:

> According to the predictions of several Christian writers, especially of such who comment upon the Apocalypse or Revelations, this year of 1666 was to prove a year of wonders, of strange revolutions in the world, and particularly, of blessing to the Jews . . .
>
> In this manner millions of people were possessed when Shabbetai Zevi first appeared at Smyrna, and published himself to the Jews for their Messiah, relating the greatness of their approaching kingdom, the strong hand whereby God was about to deliver them from bondage, and gather them from all parts of the world. It was strange to see how this fancy took and how fast the report of Shabbetai and his doctrine flew through all parts where Jews inhabited and so deeply possessed them with a belief of their new kingdom and riches, and many of them with promotion to offices of government, renown and greatness; that in all places from Constantinople to Budu (to which it was my fortune this year to travel) I perceived a strange transport in the Jews, none of them attending to any business, unless to wind up former negotiations and to prepare themselves and their families for a journey to Jerusalem. All their discourses, their dreams and disposal of their affairs tended to no other design but a re-establishment in the Land of Promise, to greatness and glory, wisdom and doctrine of the Messiah . . .
>
> An example of which is most observable in the Jews of Thessalonica, who now, full of assurance that the restoration of their kingdom and the accomplishment of the times for the coming of the Messiah was at hand . . . applied themselves immediately to fastings; and some in that manner beyond the abilities of nature, that having for the space of seven days taken no sustenance, were famished. Others buried themselves in their gardens, covering their naked bodies with earth, their hands only excepted, remained in those beds of dirt until their bodies were stiffened with cold and moisture. Others would endure to have melted wax dropped upon their shoulders; others to roll themselves in snow and throw their bodies in the coldest season of the winter into the sea or frozen waters. But the most common manner of mortification was first to prick their backs and sides with thorns and then to give themselves thirty-nine lashes. All business was laid aside. (Sir Paul Rycaut, *History of the Turkish Empire*)

There was tremendous disappointment when Shabbetai, to save his life, converted to Islam. Nonetheless, Shabbetaism survived in the Donmeh sect until the early twentieth century. Mystical speculation continued in kabbalistic circles such as the one surrounding Moses Luzzatto (1707–46):

> There is here a holy man, my master and teacher, the holy lamp, the man of God, his honour Rabbi Moses Hayyim Luzzatto. For these past two and a half years a maggid [heavenly mentor] has been revealed to him, a holy and tremendous angel who reveals wondrous mysteries to him . . . The angel speaks out of his mouth but we, like disciples, hear nothing. The angel begins to reveal great mysteries. Then my master orders Elijah to come to him and he comes to impart mysteries of his own. Sometimes Metatron, the great prince, also comes to him as well as the Faithful Shepherd [Moses], the Patriarch Abraham, Rabbi Hamnuna the Elder . . . to sum up, nothing is hidden from him. At first permission was only granted to reveal to him the mysteries of the Law, but now all things are revealed to him. (Letter of Jekuthiel Gordon)

Luzzatto described his own mystical experience:

> I fell into a trance. When I awoke, I heard a voice saying: I have descended in order to reveal the hidden secrets of the Holy King. For a while I stood there trembling, but then I took hold of myself. The voice did not cease from speaking; it imparted a particular secret to me. At the same time, on the second day, I saw to it that I was alone in the room and the voice came again to impart a further secret to me. One day he revealed to me that he was a heavenly mentor; he gave me certain letter combinations that I was to perform in order for him to come to me. I never saw him, but heard his voice speaking in my mouth . . . Then Elijah came and imparted his own secrets to me. And he said that Metatron, the Great Prince, will come to me. From that time onwards I came to remember each of my visitations – souls whose identity are revealed to me. I write down each day the new ideas each of them imparts to me. (Moses Luzzatto, letter to Benjamin Eliezer ha-Kohen Vitale)

Luzzatto's best known work was an ethical guide, *The Path of the Upright*:

> In fact, the true nature of saintliness requires much explanation. Many habits and activities are often described as examples of perfect saintliness, but are in reality only preliminary indications of this quality. People who perform these practices often lack the powers of reflection and understanding. They have not laboured to grasp the way of God clearly and unambiguously. They have tried to be saintly without thinking deeply on the matter. They have not pondered their lives or weighed themselves in the balance of wisdom. These people make saintliness profoundly unattractive for both the ordinary person and for the more intelligent. They make it appear that saintliness can be achieved by performing foolish and illogical actions such as repeating innumerable supplications and lengthy confessions, by weeping and pros-

trating oneself, by torturing oneself almost to death, perhaps by washing in snow or icy water. It may be that some of these practices do serve as penances for certain sins and others may be suitable for avowed ascetics, but they do not in themselves provide a foundation for saintliness. Saintliness itself is far more profound. It can only be cultivated through great wisdom and upon acting on truly wise motivation. Only the wise can understand the true nature of saintliness: as our Sages said: The ignorant man cannot be saintly.

Suggested Further Reading

A. Kaplan, trans., *Sefer Yetzirah (Book of Creation)*, Northvale, NJ: Jacob Aronson, 1995.

G. Scholem, *Zohar: The Book of Splendor*, New York: Schocken Books, 1995.

S. G. Kramer, *God and Man in the Sefer Hasidim*, Skokie: Hebrew Theological College Press, 1966.

G. Scholem, *Major Trends in Jewish Mysticism*, New York: Schocken Books, 1995.

Chronological Table

Circa CE	Documents	Events in Jewish History
100–200	*Sefer Yetzirah* ('Book of Creation')	
200–300	Midrash	
500–600	Babylonian Talmud	
1100–1200	HeHasid's *Book of the Pious; Book of Bahir*	Era of the Hasidei Ashkenaz
1200–1300	ben Judah's *Secret*; Abulafia's *World to Come*; ben Menahem's *Gate*; Hymn of Glory; *Zohar*	Kabbalistic Study in Provence
1500–1600	Caro's *Heavenly Mentor*, Cordovero's *Orchard* and *Pleasant Light*	Era of Safed mystics
1600–1700	Vital's *Tree, Visions* and *Gate*; Zemah's *Leader*; Rycaut's *History*	Shabbetai Zevi proclaimed Messiah
1700–1800	Gordon's letter; Luzzatto's letter and *Path of the Upright*	

9

The Hasidim and the Mitnaggdim

1. Jewry in Eastern Europe

From the thirteenth century Jews were protected in Poland and Lithuania. Here the community benefited from a system of communal authority, the Council of the Four Lands, regulating all Jewish affairs:

> A Jew who considers summoning a non-Jew before the Court of the King or before the Criminal High Court, or before the local secular courts or district courts, must, before he does anything else, present his case before the leaders of the city. Also when a non-Jew summons a Jew before the Court of the King or before the Criminal High Court, he must come before the officials of his community and listen to whatever they tell him to do. (Edicts of the Lithuanian Council, 1623)

> Everywhere where there is a market day on the Sabbath day, the local Jewish court must be careful to warn the Jews not to break the law and trade on the Sabbath. The court will teach them what is permitted and what is forbidden so that the Sabbath will not be profaned. The court shall also publicly punish all who break or dishonour the Sabbath day. (Edicts of the Lithuanian Council, 1628)

Jewish life in Eastern Europe was guided by the provisions of Joseph Caro's great legal code, the *Shulhan Arukh* ('Laid Table'), with its supplement *Mappah* ('Tablecloth') written by Moses Isserles (1525–72) for the Ashkenazim (Eastern European community):

> A Jew may not claim to be a gentile in order to avoid being killed. However, he may put on different clothes during a time of persecution so that he is not immediately recognizable as a Jew. But he may not say that he is a non-Jew . . .
>
> [Note by Isserles] It is forbidden to dress like a gentile so as not to be recognized as a Jew in order to avoid paying tolls or for similar reasons . . .
>
> It is forbidden to go before a gentile judge or a gentile law court for

trial, even if the case would be judged in accordance with Jewish law. It is forbidden even if both parties in the case agree to be tried before them. Anyone who is tried in a gentile court is a wicked man. It is as if he has scorned, blasphemed and rejected the Law of Moses, our teacher.

[Note by Isserles] Anyone who does resort to the gentile courts may be put under either the lesser or the greater ban by the Jewish courts until he has dropped the case against his opponent. A ban can also be pronounced on anyone who encourages the use of gentile courts to settle disputes. Even if the gentile courts are merely used to compel the defendant to appear at a trial before a Jewish court, such a man who resorts to them deserves to be flogged. If a man goes before a gentile court and is found guilty under the gentile laws and then turns round and insists that his opponent appear with him before a Jewish court, then some authorities would say that he should not be heard. Others argue that he should be heard unless he has caused loss to his fellow litigants in the gentile courts. I believe it is essential to follow the former ruling. (Joseph Caro, *Shulhan Arukh* with Moses Isserles' commentary)

Against this background of prosperity and security, the Chmielnicki massacres in Poland were an enormous shock:

The oppressor Chmielnicki, may his name be blotted out, heard that many Jews were gathered together in the fortress of Nemirov and that they had a great deal of gold and silver with them . . . Accordingly he sent an enemy of the Jews to lead six hundred swordsmen against this holy congregation. He also wrote to the city magistrates that this band should be given every assistance. The citizens agreed to help them with all their resources – not because they liked the Cossacks, but because they hated the Jews . . . As soon as the fortress gates were opened, the Cossacks rushed in with drawn swords and the townspeople followed them with swords, lances, scythes and even clubs. They killed a huge number of Jews. They raped the women and the young girls, although some of the women jumped into the moat near the fortress and were drowned. Many men who could swim also jumped into the water in order to swim away and escape from the slaughter. But the Russians swam after them and killed them in the water with their swords and scythes. Also some of the enemy kept shooting into the moat with their guns so that the water flowed red with blood . . . The number of those drowned and murdered in this holy congregation of Nemirov was about six thousand people. As has been described, they met all kinds of appalling deaths. May God avenge their blood! (Nathan Hannover, *The Miry Depth*)

The community was also deeply disillusioned by the conversion of

Shabbetai Zevi to Islam (see Chapter 8, Part 5):

> The news that Shabbetai had become a Turk and that the Messiah was now a Muslim spread throughout Turkey. The Jews were astounded and were very embarrassed by their own credulity and by the arguments they had used to persuade others and the converts they had made within their own families. Further afield they were generally mocked in all the towns in which they lived. Street urchins jeered after them, producing a new nickname . . . which they all would shout with contempt and scorn, pointing their fingers whenever they saw a Jew. So for a long time these deceived people remained confused and silent and they were profoundly depressed in their spirits. (Sir Paul Rycaut, *History of the Turkish Empire*)

2. The Rise of the Hasidic Movement

The founder of the Hasidic movement was Israel ben Eliezer (c. 1700–60), known as the Baal Shem Tov ('Master of the Good Name') or Besht. There are many legends about him:

> After his father's death, when the Besht was growing up, the Jews of his community were good to him because they had dearly loved his father. They sent him to a teacher for his education and he was an excellent student and made speedy progress. However, after studying for a few days, he regularly used to run away from school. They used to search for him and would find him sitting by himself in the forest. They thought he behaved like this because he had no one to look after him and was an orphan and had to make his own way. They used to bring him back to his teacher, but the same thing would happen again. He ran away to the woods to be by himself. Eventually they all gave up. They lost interest and no longer sent him to the teacher. So the boy grew up in very unusual circumstances . . .
>
> This is how he earned his living. Two or three times a week his wife used to bring a horse and waggon to him and he dug out clay for bricks. She would take it to the city and this is how she worked for him. The Besht used not to eat anything for long periods of time. When he did want to eat, he would dig a hole in the ground and put a little flour and water into the hole. This would cook in the heat of the sun. That was all he ate after fasting and he spent all his time by himself. After seven years of living like this among the mountains, the time came for him to reveal himself . . . He decided to live in the holy city of Galicia and he taught there. He could not always gather together ten men for a service in his house, but he invited a smaller number and prayed with them. He wore the very coarsest clothes and, in his poverty, his toes stuck out of the holes in his shoes. Nonetheless, he always had a ritual bath before he prayed, even on the coldest winter day, and he prayed with such concentration that sweat fell from him in great beads. Although those who were ill often visited him, he would not receive

them at first. Then one day they brought a madman (or it may have been a woman) to see him and he would not meet him. That night it was shown to him that he had passed his thirty-sixth year. He checked in the morning and found that this was correct. Then he saw the mad person and healed him . . . From then on people journeyed to see him from far and wide. *(Praises of the Besht)*

The Besht taught that sincere devotion to God was to be valued above traditional rabbinic learning:

The Besht used to say: No child is born except as the result of joy and pleasure. In the same way, if a man wants his prayers to be heard, he must offer them up with joy and pleasure.

The Besht used to say: Do not laugh at a man who gestures as he prays fervently. He gestures in order to keep himself from distracting thoughts which intrude upon him and threaten to drown his prayer. You would not laugh at a drowning man who gestures in the water in order to save himself.

The Besht used to say: Sometimes a man becomes intoxicated with ecstasy when rejoicing over the law. He feels the love of God burning within him and the words of prayer come rushing out of his mouth. He must pray quickly to keep pace with them all.

A father complained to the Besht that his son had turned away from God and asked what he should do. The Besht replied: Love him more than ever. (Aaron of Apt, *Kether Shem Tov*)

The followers of the Besht were known as the Hasidim ('pious men'). After his death the movement spread throughout Eastern Europe and beyond. Famous early Hasidic leaders included Jacob Joseph of Polonnoye, who preserved many of the Besht's sayings, and Dov Baer, the preacher of Mezeritz:

Dov Baer used to say: A father was playing with his small son and hid himself for fun. The boy looked for him and finally found him. This increased his father's love for him. In the same way, God sometimes hides himself and when, after looking for him, we eventually find him, God loves us all the more . . .

Dov Baer used to say: When a king is at a celebration, he is more approachable to many people who would otherwise not be allowed into the palace. Similarly when we approach God with joy, he is more approachable. (S. A. Horodetzky, *The Teaching of the Preacher of Mezeritz*)

Dov Baer used to say: When a child wants something from his father, the father rejoices when he can grant his son's wish. Similarly when a good man wants something, God rejoices in granting his prayer. (Letter from Rabbi Baruch of Medziboz)

The next generation of Hasidic leaders included Levi Yitshak of Berdichev, Shneur Zalman of Lyady and Elimelech of Lyzhansk:

> Levi Yitshak of Berdichev used to say: Do not despair if you preach and see no result. You can be sure that the seed you have planted will blossom in the heart of one listener. (Pinchas of Koretz, *Midrash Pinchas*)

> Shneur Zalman used to say: You can recognize a really great man by watching how he talks to ordinary people. It requires real wisdom for a learned man to talk with an ordinary man and hold his attention. (J. K. K. Rokotz, *Siach Sarfei Kodesh*)

> Elimelech of Lyzhansk used to offer the following prayer: O Lord, guard us from selfishness and from pride when we do your will. Guard us from anger and resentment, from tale-bearing and from every other evil. May no jealousy enter our hearts or the hearts of our fellowmen. Give us the power within our hearts to see no evil, but only virtue within our companions. (Y. A. Kamelhar, *Dor Deah*)

Tales of these Hasidic leaders were circulated orally among their followers. Leadership quickly became a matter of family descent and several Hasidic dynasties were founded. By the beginning of the nineteenth century, probably half of Eastern European Jewry identified with the new movement.

3. Hasidic Beliefs and Practices

Central to the philosophy of Hasidism is the doctrine of the Tsaddik, or righteous man. For the Hasidim, their Tsaddik is their spiritual ruler or mentor:

> A Hasidic follower asked the Tzanzer [Hayyim Halberstam of Lublin] whether the miracles ascribed to the Tsaddikim in such books as Stories of the Tsaddikim really occurred. The Tzanzer replied: I cannot guarantee that what is written down is true, but I am convinced that a real Tsaddik can accomplish whatever he wants provided it is in accord with the will of God. (I. Berger, *Esser Tzachtzochoth*)

> A Tsaddik fell ill and the Besht was asked by his followers to pray for him to be restored to health, but the Besht refused. A few days later, a group of brigands who had planned to raid the town were surprised and arrested by the police. The same day the Tsaddik recovered from his illness. The Besht explained that the Tsaddik's pain had caused the brigands' raid to be deferred until the police could discover them. The sufferings of a Tsaddik act like a shield. (Aaron of Apt, *Kether Shem Tov*)

Dov Baer used to explain that the Tsaddik is like the seed of the world. When a seed is planted, it draws nourishment from the earth and brings forth fruit. Similarly the Tsaddik draws forth the holy sparks from every soul and brings them heavenwards as an offering to the Creator. (Letter from Rabbi Baruch of Medziboz)

Just as the Tsaddik goes down to the doors of Hell to rescue the souls of the wicked who have retained the thought of repentance because of him, so every day, in this world, the Tsaddik goes down from his rung in order to join himself with those on a lower level . . . When he again climbs up to his rung, he brings them up with him. (Rabbi Jacob Joseph, *Toledot Ya'akov Yosef*)

Even today the leaders of the Hasidim (known as the Rebbes) are regarded with extraordinary veneration:

The Rebbes are the top-ranking religious leaders and their authority is inherited from their fathers or other close relatives. It is believed ultimately to come from God. They are beyond question of reproach. They are recognized as the 'most high who exceed, outdo and outrank every other person in the entire world'. Their entire behaviour is thought to be ritualistic. Every move or mannerism is a form of religious worship. Their ritualistic observance is the most frequent and the most intense of all worshippers. Thus the Rebbes are the core of the community.

Another example of positive control is the Rebbe's 'meal ceremonials'. During these ceremonials the Rebbe's faithful followers receive shirayim (literally leftovers) from the Rebbe's dish. The person who does not rank high in the community usually asks for shirayim by pushing his way towards the Rebbe, extending his arm and grabbing shirayim from the plate after the Rebbe moves his plate aside. But when a person is called and receives shirayim from the Rebbe's own hand, he has received one of the most coveted honours in the community. (Solomon Poll, *The Hasidic Community of Williamsburg*)

The Hasidim adopted a new prayer book, based on the prayer book of Isaac Luria (see Chapter 8, Part 4):

I asked my master, my father, my teacher and my guide (May his light continue to shine!) why we have changed the standard version of the Prayer Book. He replied: Look, Joseph Caro (of blessed memory), who is the most important of all the codifiers (of blessed memory) quotes Luria's version. Afterwards Moses Isserles (of blessed memory), who is also the most important codifier, came and introduced the rules for the people of Israel. He saw what great light there is in Luria's version — it is so bright that the world is unworthy of it — so he established the Ashkenazic [traditional Eastern

European Jewish] version which is suitable for ordinary people. But he never intended to stop the Tsaddikim who are purified from all uncleanness and strict to the last hair breadth from using the version of Joseph Caro (of blessed memory). (Rabbi Elimelech, *Noam Elimelekh*)

Hasidic prayer is notable for its enthusiasm and intensity:

> The Hasidim . . . say that the feelings and burning enthusiasm of our teacher R. Issachar Dov were indescribable. The mood reached its peak when he recited the 'Out of the Deep' prayer before the shofar [ram's horn] was blown. While he was reciting one verse, he wept bitterly so that the heart of everyone present melted like water. Then directly afterwards, he recited the next verse with such exaltation and joy that it was difficult to believe that only a minute before he had been in tears. He poured out his soul in prayer like a son longs for his father and it went directly to the heart of all his fellow worshippers. At that moment they reached a spiritual height that they could never have achieved through their own efforts. (Description of the third Tsaddik of Belz)

The European Hasidic communities were decimated in the Holocaust (see Chapter 12, Part 2). Extraordinary tales were told of their bravery:

> The Grand Rebbe of Bobov and his family were among the two thousand Jews arrested in Lvov. Four days later, Rabbi Ben-Zion Halberstam, dressed in his silk Sabbath kaftan and his tall fur hat, marched to his death. He was urged to escape, but he replied: One does not run away from the sound of the Messiah's footsteps, and he continued to walk with his dignified stride in the direction of Janow, where the open pits in the forest were waiting. He was murdered by the Nazis and their Ukrainian collaborators. May his sainted memory be blessed. (Adapted from Yaffa Eliach, *Hasidic Tales of the Holocaust*)

However, Hasidic groups survive today particularly in Israel and the United States. They are readily visible by their dress and demeanour:

> A man goes by with a briefcase, intent and absorbed. Because hair is worn longer now, his side-curls seem less exotic than in former times, though they owe little to fashion. His black silk coat gives him an important look. What is he? . . . He is a follower of the great Jewish mystic who lived in Poland in the eighteenth century who sought God in the solitude of the Carpathian mountains, but discovered him in the joy of his own heart. He does not seem very joyous, you'd exclaim. Ah, but wait till you see him in synagogue, dancing and swaying with the scroll! (Lionel Blue, *To Heaven with the Scribes and Pharisees*)

4. The Vilna Gaon and the Mitnaggdim

The traditionalist opponents of the Hasidim were known as the Mitnaggdim ('Opponents'). Prominent among them was Elijah ben Solomon Zalman (1720–97), known as the Vilna Gaon:

> There is another story about the greatest rabbi of his time – Elijah, the Gaon of Vilna. In the eighteenth century the learned rabbi was giving a tutorial. Two of his pupils looked out of the window at a bird soaring in the sky. He asked one of them: What were you thinking as you watched the bird? The boy replied: I was thinking of the soul soaring to Heaven. Elijah asked the boy to leave the class; he smelt the mysticism of Jewish Poland. He turned to the other boy and asked him the same question. The boy considered: If that bird dropped dead and fell between two fences, who would own the body? His teacher replied: God be praised for someone who knows what religion is about! (Adapted from Lionel Blue, *To Heaven with the Scribes and Pharisees*)

In 1772, under Elijah's influence, the Jews of Vilna issued edicts against the Hasidim. According to the Hasidim, the Hasidic leaders showed great forbearance:

> When conflict broke out between the Hasidim and the Mitnaggdim, Rabbi Elijah of Vilna did not argue the matter out. He issued a decree of expulsion against those who followed the Hasidic way and put them all under a ban of excommunication. When Rabbi Dov Baer heard this, he quoted the Law to his disciples: Our enemies follow the Commandment You shall remove evil from your midst. [Deuteronomy 21: 21]. We will follow another commandment: You shall not take revenge or bear malice [Leviticus 19: 18]. Rabbi Dov Baer summarized the teachings of the Hasidim in the two maxims, Love God and Love Man. He forbade his followers from indulging in bitter arguments. When eventually, in despair, they issued their own ban against their oppressors, the Rabbi was so upset that he fell seriously ill. He did not live to see the full conflict. (Chaim Bloch, *Gemeinde der Chassidim*)

The Vilna Gaon could not tolerate the exuberance of the new movement, believing that it undermined stringent scholarship and was reminiscent of the excesses of Shabbetai Zevi and his followers (see Chapter 8, Part 5):

> Satan realized that Schneur Zalman had been very successful in spreading Hasidism among the Jews of Lithuania and decided to combat his work by

arousing quarrels. He encouraged some of the Hasidim to become over-enthusiastic, to shout their prayers, to insult traditionalist yeshivah students, to dance in the street and to roll around on the ground. This made the Vilna Gaon very angry . . . He excommunicated the Hasidim without even listening to their defence. (M. Indritz, *Be-Ohelei Habad*)

The ban was the first of many:

As a result of our sins, wicked and worthless men known as the Hasidim have left the Jewish fold and have set up their own places of worship. As everyone knows, they conduct their services in a mad and unseemly fashion, following different rituals which do not conform to the teachings of our holy Law . . . The exaggerations and miracle tales which are described in their books are clear and obvious lies and . . . there is even a move to disregard the obligations of the Law of Moses . . . The following are the protective measures agreed at our meeting:
1. We order a fast and public prayer to be kept on 25 Tevet of this year . . .
2. Every effort should be made to end the prayer meetings of the heretics . . .
3. Careful watch should be kept to ensure that no one studies their literature . . .
4. The validity of the ordinances proclaimed in Brody and Vilna are confirmed . . .
5. The animals killed by their ritual slaughterers may not be eaten. It is to be regarded as carrion . . .
6. No one is to shelter any member of the Hasidim . . .
7. No member of the Hasidim may bring a suit in a Jewish court, nor hold a position as Cantor, Rabbi or, as goes without saying, as teacher of children . . .
8. All information, both good and bad, about the Hasidim must be brought to the attention of the court. (Decree of the Shklov Community, 1786)

The Vilna Gaon was also an outstanding talmudic scholar. He disapproved of pilpul (casuistic hairsplitting in the interpretation of the text):

Through pilpul sin increases, wickedness grows, pleasant speech disappears and truth is driven away from the congregation of the Lord. (Introduction to his *Commentary on the Shulhan Arukh*)

He also had strong views on the education of the young:

Bring up your sons in the right way with gentleness. They should have a teacher constantly in the house who should be generously paid . . . Pay especial attention to the children's diet and health so that they do not lack anything. First they should study the five books of Moses, almost learning them by heart. But do not let the teacher impose his yoke too heavily on them. Teaching is only effective when it is given easily and happily. Give the children little presents of money and suchlike to give them pleasure since this helps them in their studies. Please give their education your unfailing attention; everything else is unimportant. (Elijah ben Solomon, *Testament*)

As a result of his efforts, a rich Jewish culture grew up in Lithuania which rejected the emotionalism of Hasidism in favour of serious scholarship and was characterized by a wry sense of humour. This is preserved to this day in traditional Yiddish jokes:

A Litvak is so clever that he repents before he sins.

A melamed [teacher of young children] declared: If I were a Rockefeller, I'd be richer than a Rockefeller – I'd do a little teaching on the side. (Adapted from Leo Rosten, *The Joys of Yiddish*)

5. The Shtetl, the Yeshivah and the Musar Movement

A shtetl was a small town predominantly inhabited by Jews and it provided the regular pattern of living for the Jews of Eastern Europe from the seventeenth to the late nineteenth centuries:

Amid thick forests and deep swamps on the slope of a hill, level at the summit, lay the village of Frampol. Nobody knew who had founded it, or why just there. Goats grazed among the tombstones which were already sunk in the ground of the cemetery. In the community house there was a parchment with a chronicle on it, but the first page was missing and the writing had faded. Legends were current among the people, tales of wicked intrigue concerning a mad nobleman, a lascivious lady, a Jewish scholar and a wild dog. But their true origin was lost in the past.

Peasants who tilled the surrounding countryside were poor; the land was stubborn. In the village Jews were impoverished, their roofs were straw, their floors dirt. In the summer many of them wore no shoes and in cold weather they wrapped their feet in rags or wore sandals made of straw.

Rabbi Ozier, although renowned for his erudition, received a salary of only eighteen grozy a week. The assistant rabbi, besides being ritual slaughterer, was teacher, matchmaker, bath-attendant and poorhouse nurse as well. Even those villagers who were considered wealthy knew little of luxury. They wore cotton gaberdines tied about their waists with string and tasted meat only on the Sabbath. Gold coin was rarely seen in Frampol. (Isaac Bashevis Singer, *The Gentleman from Crakow*)

There was little privacy in the shtetl. Everyone knew everyone's business and marriages were formally arranged by the shadchan (matchmaker) of whom innumerable anecdotes were told:

A shadchan sang the praises of a particular girl and brought a male client to see her. The young man was horrified. 'You said she was young and she's at least forty,' he complained. 'You said she was beautiful, but she looks like a duck. You said she was shapely and she's big enough for two. You said . . .'
 'You don't have to whisper,' said the shadchan, 'She's also hard of hearing.' (Adapted from Leo Rosten, *The Joys of Yiddish*)

Jewish education began at the chedar or elementary school:

I should now describe the general state of Jewish schools. Usually the school is housed in a small, smoky hut and the children sit either on benches or on the bare earth. The schoolmaster, in a dirty shirt, sits on the table and grips between his knees a bowl in which he beats tobacco into snuff with a huge pestle like the club of Hercules. At the same time he asserts his authority over the children. In each corner, the undermasters give lessons and rule their small charges quite as tyrannously as the master himself. These gentlemen keep the largest share of the breakfast, lunch and other food sent in for themselves and sometimes the boys get nothing at all. But they do not dare to complain because they are frightened of exciting the anger of these despots. The children are imprisoned here from morning until night. They have no time for themselves except an afternoon on Friday and at the new moon. (Solomon Maimon, *Autobiography*)

After chedar, if at all possible, families sent their sons to a yeshivah (academy) to study Talmud:

He explained that he was returning to Beshev for his fourth year. The yeshivah there was small with only thirty students and the people in the town provided board for them all. The food was plentiful and the housewives darned the students' socks and took care of their laundry. The Beshev rabbi, who headed the yeshivah, was a genius. He could pose ten questions and answer all ten with one proof. Most of the students eventually found wives in the town . . . The students at the yeshivah studied in pairs and Avigdor chose Anshel for a partner . . . The two friends, sharing a lectern in the corner of the study house, spent more time talking than learning . . . The friends met twice each day; in the morning they studied the Gemara and the commentaries and in the afternoon the legal codes and their glosses . . . Anshel spoke in a singsong, gesticulated with her thumb, clutched her sidelocks, plucked at her beardless chin and made all the customary gestures of a yeshivah student. In the heat of the argument she even seized Avigdor by the lapel and called him stupid . . . Dusk fell and the two began to recite the evening prayer. In his confusion Avigdor mixed up the blessings, omitted some and repeated others. He glanced sideways at Anshel who was rocking back and forth, beating her breast and bowing her head. (Adapted from Isaac Bashevis Singer, *Yentl the Yeshivah Boy*)

The Hasidim and the Mitnaggdim supported different yeshivot. In the nineteenth century, particularly in Lithuania, Musar (ethics) was added to the curriculum by Rabbi Israel Lipkin.

The busy man is always doing evil. When he does badly in business, his mind and strength grow confused and he becomes subject to the chains of trouble and distress. Therefore on the holy Sabbath set a time to gather together . . . the city's important men for the study of ethics. The others will follow . . . Through quiet reflection and careful thought everyone will strengthen his fellow, end his lazy ways and cure the follies of his heart. (Israel Lipkin, letter to the Vilna Community)

Ever since I was fortunate enough to enjoy the great light provided by the light of the world, my master and teacher of blessed memory (Rabbi Israel Lipkin), I began to understand a little of the science of Musar. It is the only science (in addition to the wisdom of our Law, which lies waiting for all to pick up) that can help someone wage the battle of our Law, that is, the battle against our own human nature, against our brutal animal natures. It is a tremendous struggle to bring the huge force of human nature under the influence of reason. The soldiers are few and are becoming fewer all the time, while brute nature seems to be increasing in power. If man is to overcome his own nature, he needs not only courage, but also the ability to recognize the cunning ways in which men are trapped and misled by the evil inclination. All this is included in the science of Musar. (Simhah Broida, *Wisdom and Understanding*)

Suggested Further Reading

M. Buber, *Tales of the Hasidim* (2 vols.), New York: Schocken Books, 1995.

I. Cohen, *History of the Jews of Vilna*, Philadelphia: Jewish Publication Society, 1943.

L. J. Newman and S. Spitz, *The Hasidic Anthology*, New York: C. Scribner's Sons, 1934.

M. Samuel, *The World of Sholom Aleichem*, New York: Alfred A. Knopf, 1944.

Chronological Table

Circa CE	Documents	Events in Jewish History
1500–1600	Caro's *Shulhan Arukh;* Isserles' *Mappah*	Council of the Four Lands administer Eastern European Jewry
1600–1700	Council edicts; Hannover's *Miry Depth;* Rycaut's *History*	Chmielnicki massacres Shabbetai Zevi declared messiah
1700–1800	Aaron of Apt's *Kether,* Joseph's *Toledot;* Elimelech's *Noam;* Shklov decree; ben Solomon's *Commentary* and *Testament;* Maimon's *Autobiography*	Rise of Hasidism Opposition of Mitnaggdim
1800–1900	*Praises of the Besht;* Baruch's letters; Pinchas' *Midrash;* Lipkin's letter; Broida's *Wisdom*	Mass emigration to USA
1900–	Horodetzky's *Teaching;* Rokotz' *Siach;* Kamelhar's *Dor,* Berger's *Esser,* Poll's *Hasidic Community;* Eliach's *Hasidic Tales;* Blue's *To Heaven;* Bloch's *Gemeinde;* Indritz's *Be-Ohelei;* Rosten's *Joys;* Singer's *Gentleman* and *Yentl*	Holocaust Establishment of the State of Israel

10

The Enlightenment and Progressive Judaism

1. The Jewish Community in Western Europe

By the late eighteenth century, some Christian writers in Western and Central Europe were advocating tolerance for the Jews:

> Only common people believe that it is permissible to deceive a Jew or accuse him of being permitted by his law to deceive non-Jews. It is only bigoted clergy who have collected tales of the prejudices of the Jews which are used to reinforce their own prejudices . . . Jews have wisdom; they are intelligent and hard-working and dogged. They are capable of finding their own way in every situation . . . Although . . . they have a strong tendency to be on the lookout for every sort of gain and they love usury . . . These defects are made worse in many of them by their self-imposed isolation which is based on their religious laws and on rabbinic sophistry . . . If our arguments are correct, we shall find the oppression under which they suffer and the trade restrictions imposed on them are the real reason for their shortcomings. Therefore it follows that we have also discovered the means by which their faults may be cured and by which they will become both better human beings and more useful citizens. (Wilhelm Christian Dohm, *Concerning the Amelioration of the Civil Status of Jews*)

The Holy Roman Emperor Joseph II agreed with this view and in 1781 he issued an edict of toleration:

> In order to make the Jews more useful, discriminatory Jewish clothing which has been worn in the past is now abolished. Within two years the Jews must abandon their own language; from now on all their contracts, bonds, wills, accounts, ledgers, certificates and any legally binding document must be drawn up in German . . . Jews may continue to use their own language during religious services . . . Jews who do not have the opportunity of sending their children to Jewish schools must send them to Christian ones to learn reading, writing, arithmetic and other subjects . . . Jews will also be permitted to attend the imperial universities . . . Leaders of local commu-

nities must rationally instruct their people that the Jews may be treated like any other fellow human being. There must be an end to the prejudice and contempt which some subjects, particularly the less intelligent, have shown towards the Jewish people. (Edict of Joseph II)

In 1806 the Emperor Napoleon of France convened an Assembly of Jewish Notables. The question at issue was whether Jews could be full citizens of the host countries:

Questions addressed to the Assembly by His Majesty the King and Emperor:
Do Jews born in France and treated by the law as French citizens, acknowledge France as their country? Do they feel obliged to defend it? Must they keep its laws and follow all the provisions of the Civil Code?
Answer of the Assembly:
Men who have adopted a country and who have lived there for many generations and who, even when certain of the country's laws have curtailed their civil rights, are so attached to it that they prefer the misfortune of civil disability to that of leaving, must be seen in France as Frenchmen. Jews regard the obligation of defending France as both an honourable and a precious duty. Jeremiah 29 strongly recommends the Jews to see Babylon as their country, even though they were only to stay there for seventy years. He tells them to cultivate the fields, to build houses, to sow and to plant. The Jews followed his advice to such an extent that, according to Ezra 2, when Cyrus allowed them to return to Jerusalem to rebuild the Temple, only forty-two thousand, three hundred and sixty of them left Babylon. Mostly it was the poor people who went; the rich stayed in Babylon.
Love of one's country is an entirely natural and lively sentiment among the Jews. It is completely in harmony with their religious beliefs that a French Jew in England feels himself to be a stranger, even in the company of English Jews. English Jews feel the same in France. Their patriotism is so great that in the last war French Jews could be found fighting against Jews of other countries with which France was at war. Many of them were honourably wounded and others won on the field of battle fervent testimonies to their valour. (Record of the Assembly of Jewish Notables, 1806)

As a result of the assembly, Napoleon revived the institution of the Sanhedrin. Not all reactions were favourable. In 1807 the Holy Synod of the Russian Orthodox Church ordered the following proclamation to be read in all its churches:

In order to complete the degradation of the Church, [Napoleon] has convened the Jewish synagogues of France, restored the dignity of the rabbis and laid the foundation of a new Hebrew Sanhedrin, the same notorious tribunal which dared to condemn Our Lord and Saviour Jesus Christ to the cross. He now has the audacity to gather together all of the Jews whom God, in his anger, had scattered over the face of the earth, and launch all of them into the destruction of Christ's Church. O unspeakable presumption! Greater than any appalling crime that they should proclaim Napoleon as the Messiah! (Edict of the Russian Church, 1807)

After Napoleon's defeat at Waterloo in 1815 there was an attempt to turn the clock back. There were serious anti-Jewish riots in Germany, but, increasingly, liberal views began to prevail. Heinrich Heine, who was himself a baptized Jew, correctly read the signs of the times:

> What is the great question of the age? It is Emancipation! Not just the emancipation of the Irish, the Greeks, the Jews of Frankfurt, the Negroes of the West Indies or of other oppressed groups, but the emancipation of the whole world . . . which even now is pulling away from the leading strings of the aristocracy and the privileged classes. (Heinrich Heine, *Germany*)

2. The Haskalah

The roots of the Haskalah (the Jewish Enlightenment) go back to seventeenth-century Holland. The Dutch community was secure, rich and cultured. Most famous of the Dutch Jewish thinkers of the period was Baruch Spinoza. He suggested that the Pentateuch was not entirely composed by Moses and that the Jews were not necessarily the Chosen People of God. In consequence he was excommunicated from the synagogue. Nonetheless his ideas were revived by later thinkers:

> Therefore when scripture exhorts the Jews to keep the Law, insists that God has chosen them for himself before all the other nations (Deut. 10: 15); that he is near to them, but not near to others (Deut. 4: 7); that he has given his righteous Law to them alone (Deut. 4: 8) and that he has singled them out from all the others (Deut. 4: 32), it is only speaking according to its hearers' understanding who . . . as Moses indicated (Deut. 9: 6–7) did not know true blessedness. For in fact they would have been just as present to them if he had been equally present to others. The Law would have had the same measure of righteousness if it had been ordained for all and the Jews themselves would have been just as wise. God's miracles would have demonstrated his power just as effectively if they had been done for other nations as well and finally the Jews would have had exactly the same obligation to worship God if he had given his gifts equally to everyone. (Baruch Spinoza, *Tractatus Theologico-Politicus*)

Moses Mendelssohn, a friend of the Christian philosopher G. E. Lessing, proved to be the most influential thinker of the Haskalah. He worked tirelessly for freedom of conscience in religion:

For the sake of a happier posterity, at least pave the way to the height of civilization, to the universal tolerance among men for which reason is longing
in vain. Do not reward or punish any doctrinal belief. Do not hold out bribes
or incentives to encourage people to adopt particular theologies. Allow
everyone who does not disturb the peace, who keeps the law of the land
and who acts righteously towards you and your fellow countrymen to say
what he thinks. Allow him to pray to God in his own way, or in the way of
his forefathers and let him seek eternal salvation wherever he thinks he may
find it. Do not let anyone be an investigator of hearts or a judge of opinions in your states. Do not let anyone usurp a right which the Omniscient
has reserved for himself. As long as we render to Caesar the things that are
Caesar's and you yourself render to God the things that are God's. Love truth.
Love peace. (Moses Mendelssohn, *Jerusalem*)

Among his many projects, Mendelssohn translated the Pentateuch into
German:

We the People of God are scattered in all the lands of Greater Germany and
we grew up under the influence of the language of the dominant people.
The ways of our holy language have been forgotten among us, the melody
of its phrasing eludes us and the beauty of its poetry is now hidden from our
eyes. No one has taken pains to translate our Torah into German as it is spo-
ken today among our own people. (Moses Mendelssohn, *Alim li-Terufa*)

Mendelssohn also encouraged the modernization of Jewish education to
include the teaching of secular culture. He advised his co-religionists:

Adopt the customs and constitution of the country in which you live, but
also be careful to follow the religion of your fathers. As well as you can, you
must carry both burdens. It is not easy because, on the one hand, people
make it hard for you to carry the burden of civil life because of your faithfulness to your religion and, on the other hand, the climate of the times
makes keeping religious law harder than it need be in some respects.
Nevertheless, you must try. Stand fast in the place you have been allocated
by Providence and submit to everything that happens to you as you were
commanded long ago by your law giver. Indeed, I do not understand how
those who are part of the household of Jacob can with a good conscience
not fully observe the Jewish law. (Moses Mendelssohn, *Jerusalem*)

Followers of Moses Mendelssohn and the Haskalah were known as the
Maskilim. Their ideas spread from Germany, through the Austrian empire,
to Galicia, Lithuania and Russia. They promoted a revival of the Hebrew

language, wrote for scholarly Hebrew journals and spread modern European culture among the Jews:

> It was then that the Haskalah movement among the Jews blossómed. In the past people had been kept in darkness about all secular knowledge, but they saw a great light in the person of Moses Mendelssohn. He combined Torah, wisdom and reverence for God. His friendship with Lessing gave him great fame in Germany and he was considered to be an important German scholar. He was a model for young Jews who envied his renown and they began to study foreign languages and history and formed study circles among themselves.
>
> When Mendelssohn had translated the Pentateuch into German, many people wanted to translate the whole Bible, which they subsequently accomplished. The whole system of study was completely changed and there was a new spirit among the young people. Anyone who wants to have some understanding of the current spirit in Germany, particularly in Prussia, need only look at our present situation here in Russia today.
>
> In that chaotic time of transition from one way of life to another . . . Mendel Lefin's works were most beneficial, for he opened the eyes of many and made knowledge increase. In my youth, I knew many people who had been inspired to seek learning by Mendel Lefin's Hebrew translations, which they read as manuscripts. From this they were encouraged to educate their children and teach them foreign languages. If the reader has any idea of the obscurantism of the region of Podolia of that time, then he will understand the extent of Lefin's achievements . . .
>
> All the while the Maskilim in Odessa busied themselves through storm and stress to increase education and knowledge in the land and lighten the darkness that surrounded our people in Russia. There was great tumult in Jewish circles, like the roaring waves of the ocean in a storm and there was a bitter struggle between the left and the right. (Abraham Ber Gottlober, *Memoirs*)

3. The Growth of the Reform Movement

As a result of the Haskalah, Jews were no longer insulated from the currents of European civilization. At the beginning of the nineteenth century a programme of religious reform was initiated and the first Reform Temple was opened in Seesen in 1810. The address of its founder, Isaac Jacobson at the opening ceremony has been preserved:

> Let me be frank my brothers, our ritual is weighed down with religious customs, which are offensive both to reason and to our Christian friends. The sacredness of our religion is desecrated and the reasonable man dishonoured if too much emphasis is put upon such customs. On the other hand a man is greatly respected if he encourages himself and his friends to dispense with

them . . . And you, my other greatly honoured friends, who do not share some aspects of my faith and identify yourselves by a different name, I hope I have the full agreement of your sympathetic hearts for the principles behind this Temple building and for our hopes for a happier future for my co-religionists. Our intentions in no way contradict the principles of pure religion, the demands of reason, general morality or your own humanitarian attitude. Therefore I am sure that you will receive my brothers warmly, that you will not reject them, as too often your ancestors did, but instead that you will lovingly accept them into your business and social circles. (Isaac Jacobson, Dedication Address)

Another Reform Temple was founded in Hamburg in 1818 where the congregation issued its own prayer book:

Public worship has for some time been neglected by too many because there is less and less knowledge of the language in which it is traditionally conducted and also because many other corruptions have crept in over the years. Because of this, the undersigned, convinced of the necessity of restoring public worship to its proper place and dignity, have combined to follow the example of several Israelitish congregations, particularly the one in Berlin. They plan to arrange in this city, together with others of a like mind, a dignified and orderly ritual according to which services will be conducted on the Sabbath, on holy days and on other solemn occasions. They will be conducted in their own Temple, especially built for this purpose. Specifically a German sermon, choral singing and an organ accompaniment will be introduced.

Incidentally these rituals will not be limited to Temple services. They will be applied to all the ritual activities and acts of daily life which are blessed by the Church or by their own nature. Outstanding among these are the admission of the new-born into the covenant of the fathers, weddings and similar. In addition a religious ceremony will be introduced in which both boys and girls, after receiving sufficient religious instruction, will be confirmed in the faith of Moses. (Constitution of the Hamburg Temple)

The Orthodox were unequivocal in their condemnation of this new movement:

It is forbidden to change anything in the order of prayer as it was handed down to us from earliest times.
It is forbidden in the synagogue to pray in any language except the holy language, as has been used in all Israel.
It is forbidden to play on any musical instrument in the synagogue either on Sabbath or on holidays, even if the player is not a Jew.
(*These Are the Words of the Covenant*, issued by the traditional rabbis of Europe)

Many of the early German Reform rabbis were involved in the scientific study of Judaism (*Wissenschaft des Judentums*), an attempt to study the tradition with no religious preconceptions. This was a direct challenge to the Orthodox belief that both written and oral law were of divine origin:

> Contents of volume I of the *Journal for the Science of Judaism:*
> - On the Idea of a Science of Judaism. Immanuel Wolf
> - Legislation Concerning the Jews of Rome According to Roman Legal Sources. Dr Eduard Gans
> - Letters on the Reading of Holy Scripture with a Translation of Micah VI and VII. David Friedlander
> - Lectures on the History of the Jews in Northern Europe and in Slavic Countries. Dr Eduard Gans
> - On the Belief of the Jews in the Coming of the Messiah. Lazarus Bendavid
> - Simon ben Isaac Called Rashi. Dr Zunz
> - On the Natural Aspect of the Jewish State. Ludwig Markus
> - Basic Outlines of the Mosaic–Talmudic Law of Inheritance. Eduard Gans
> - On Written and Oral Law. Lazarus Bendavid
> - On the Empiric Psychology of the Jews in the Age of the Talmud. L. Bernhardt
> - Basic Outlines of a Future Statistic of the Jew. Dr Zunz. (*Journal for the Science of Judaism*, 1822)

The *Journal for the Science of Judaism* only lasted a year, but it was succeeded in 1835 by a new publication, the *Scientific Journal for Jewish Theology*, edited by Abraham Geiger:

> Beyond external emancipation, there is the inner emancipation which will be the subject of our columns. Our ultimate goal is to awaken the spirit of our fellow Jews and, where it has been awakened, to inspire and ennoble it and to call it back from the pernicious ways of indifference. This is what we are hoping to achieve and this is the purpose and aim of this magazine. We are concerned with both the beliefs and the ethics of Jews and the Jewish religion. (Abraham Geiger, *The Scientific Journal for Jewish Theology*)

Reform Judaism spread from Germany to England and in 1841 the West London Synagogue was founded:

> Not, then, to weaken, but to strengthen our faith; not to trespass against, but to consolidate the great principles of that law which our fathers tremblingly heard amongst the thunders of Sinai – this synagogue has been established. Our unerring guide has been and will continue to be, the sacred volume of the scriptures; by that alone have we endeavoured to regulate our

principles. In matters relating to public worship, we desire to reject nothing that bears the stamp of antiquity, when that stamp is genuine and in accordance with the revealed will of God; nor to condemn anything because it is new, provided the newness of the measure be consonant with the spirit of the religion given us by the Almighty through Moses; a religion so framed to adapt itself to all our destinies, in all their various places, whether politically glorious on the throne of David, or politically prostrate in the thraldom of dispersion. (David Frank, Dedication Sermon, West London Synagogue)

4. The Development of Reform Judaism in the United States

As early as 1824 Jews of German origin had tried to introduce services similar to those of the Hamburg Temple in Charleston, South Carolina:

Our desire is to yield everything to the feeling of the truly pious Israelite, but to take away everything that might excite the disgust of the well-informed Israelite. To throw away rabbinical interpolations; to avoid useless repetition; to read or chant with solemnity; to recite such portions of the Pentateuch and the Prophets, as custom and practice have appointed to be read in the original Hebrew; but to follow such selections with a translation in English, and a lecture or discourse upon the Law, explanatory to its meaning, edifying to the young, gratifying to the old, and instructive to every age and class of society. (Isaac Harby, lecture on the first anniversary of the founding of the Charleston Society)

By the middle of the century, the need for an American rabbinical college was being discussed:

We ought to be American Israelites, i.e., Americans as men and citizens and Israelites in our religion . . . If this truth was acknowledged we would be united at one; and if our ministers were thoroughly Americanized the fact would successfully be urged upon the people. Let us educate our ministers here, in our own college, and we will soon have American ministers, American congregations, and an American Union of Israelites for religious and charitable purposes. Let us have American-trained teachers, and they will educate for us American citizens. (Isaac M. Wise, Appeal, 1854)

The Hebrew Union College was eventually established in 1875. Initially it was intended to represent all shades of American Jewish opinion. Unfortunately a gala banquet celebrating the ordination of the first graduates contained tref (ritually unclean) food, which led to the withdrawal of the traditionalists:

> The Reverend I. M. Wise, President of the Hebrew Union College, and ordainer of four rabbis, has not yet thought fit to protest against the clam–frog–crab banquet tendered by the Jews of Cincinnati to the Jewish ministers and laymen . . . We know that the laws of forbidden food have been taught to the graduating class! What at admirable closing commentary thereunto was furnished by the spectacle of these teachers devouring the abominations of Talmud. (Frederick de Sola Mendes, Protest, 1883)

The principles of Reform Judaism in the United States were established at a rabbinical conference in Pittsburgh in 1885. These came to be known at the Pittsburgh Platform:

> First . . . We hold that Judaism presents the highest conception of the God-idea as taught in our holy scriptures and developed and spiritualized by the Jewish teachers in accordance with the moral and philosophical progress of their respective ages . . .
>
> Second . . . We hold that the modern discoveries of scientific researches in the domains of nature and history are not antagonistic to the doctrines of Judaism, the Bible reflecting the primitive ideas of its own age and at times clothing its conception of divine providence and justice dealing with man in miraculous narratives.
>
> Third . . . Today we accept as binding only the moral laws and maintain only such ceremonies as elevate and sanctify our lives, but reject all such as are not adapted to the views and habits of modern civilization.
>
> Fourth . . . We hold that all such Mosaic and rabbinical laws as regulate diet, priestly purity and dress originated in ages and under the influence of ideas altogether foreign to our present mental and spiritual state . . . Their observance in our day is apt rather to obstruct than to further modern spiritual elevation.
>
> Fifth . . . We consider ourselves no longer a nation but a religious community, and therefore expect neither a return to Palestine, nor a sacrificial worship under the administration of the sons of Aaron, nor the restoration of any of the laws concerning the Jewish state.
>
> Sixth . . . We recognize in Judaism a progressive religion, ever striving to be in accord with the postulates of reason . . . We acknowledge that the spirit of broad humanity of our age is our ally in the fulfilment of our mission, and therefore we extend the hand of fellowship to all who co-operate with us in the establishment of the reign of truth and righteousness among men.
>
> Seventh . . . We reassert the doctrine of Judaism, that the soul of man is immortal . . . We reject as ideas not rooted in Judaism the belief both in bodily resurrection and in Gehenna and Eden, as abodes for everlasting punishment or reward.

Eight . . . In full accord with the spirit of Mosaic legislation, which strives to regulate the relation between rich and poor, we deem it our duty to participate in the great task of modern times, to solve on the basis of justice and righteousness the problems presented by the contrasts and evils of the present organization of society.

By the end of the century Reform Judaism was firmly established both in Europe and the United States. In 1894 the Central Conference of American Rabbis, the Reform rabbinical association, published the Union Prayer Book which, with modifications, remained the standard prayer book for the American Reform movement until the late twentieth century:

> The synagogue is the sanctuary of Israel. It was born out of Israel's longing for the living God. It has been to Israel throughout his endless wanderings a visible token of the presence of God in the midst of the people. It has shed a beauty which is the beauty of holiness and has ever stood on the high places as the champion of justice and brotherhood and peace. It is Israel's sublime gift to the world. Its truths are true for all men, its love is a love for all men, its God is the God of all men even as was prophesied of old. My house shall be called a house of prayer for all peoples. Come then, ye who inherit and ye who share the fellowship of Israel, ye who hunger for righteousness, ye who seek the Lord of Hosts, come and together let us lift up our hearts in worship. (Union Prayer Book)

5. Opposition to Reform

From the start, traditionalists were appalled by the Reform movement. The responsum of the Beth Din (rabbinical court) of Prague to the new Reform Temple of Hamburg in 1819 was typical:

> In fact, these people have no religion at all. All they want to do is to show off before the Christians as being more learned than other Jews. Fundamentally they are neither Christians or Jews. Playing the organ on the Holy Sabbath is, in every way, against Jewish law, even if the musician is a non-Jew . . . It is not permitted to follow the precepts of that blasphemous book Nogah Tsedek, published in Dessau. We are aware that certain people are being paraded with much pomp in this book, but the whole thing is lies and deceit. It aims to deceive with meaningless words. In short, any alteration to the prayers and customs which were handed down to us by our forefathers is contrary to Jewish law. (Responsum of the Beth Din of Prague collected in *These are the Words of the Covenant*)

Opposition continued throughout the century. Even Rabbi Solomon

Rapoport, who was leader of the Haskalah in Eastern Europe, was unequivocal in his condemnation:

> What must we do to protect ourselves against these people? We must follow the example of our forefathers and see what they did against heretical sects which tried to destroy rabbinic Judaism. We must insist that our fellow Jews have no social intercourse with the members of this Reform association and, in particular, they must not intermarry with them. That is how it was done in the past with the Samaritans, Sadducees, Karaites and Saruans. Complete separation must be maintained. If it is not, many disadvantages will follow, since they reject our tradition and interpret the Laws of Moses according to their own whim or convenience. (Solomon Rapoport in *Rabbinic Opinions*, ed. Solomon A. Trier)

When members of the Frankfurt Reform association encouraged the abandonment of circumcision, the Orthodox rabbi, Solomon A. Trier was aghast:

> A Jewish citizen in this city neglected to have his healthy newborn son circumcized. As soon as I discovered this, I tried every possible persuasion to keep the father from this open defiance of Judaism . . . Neither fatherly advice nor rational argument made any difference . . . Now the long-suspected secret aim of the so-called Reform association, which has been flourishing in the dark, is brought to light in this public rejection of the sign of the membership of our faith. The intentions of this association can be seen clearly by everyone; it wants to eliminate what is an unquestioned Jewish law. They claim it is out of date in modern religious practice. (Solomon A. Trier, ed., *Rabbinic Opinions*)

The Reformers countered the criticism of the Orthodox with equal harshness:

> What did most of the old rabbis do who were our immediate predecessors . . . ? Nothing! What did they do for morality and the edification of their congregations? Nothing! What did they do for the schools? Nothing! What for community service? Nothing! What for the rooting out of prejudice against people who had different opinions . . . ? Nothing! Absolutely nothing! (Joseph Kahn in *Rabbinic Opinions*, ed. Bernhard Wechsler)

Most influential among the German Orthodox thinkers was Samson Raphael Hirsch, who is generally regarded as being the founder of the Neo-Orthodox movement. When a new seminary was proposed in Breslau in 1853, Hirsch sent the following questions to its founder, Zacharias Frankel:

1. What will Revelation mean in the proposed seminary? Orthodox Judaism teaches the divine origin of the whole Bible . . .
2. What will the Bible mean in the proposed seminary? Orthodox Judaism teaches the divine origin of the whole Bible . . .
3. What will tradition mean in the proposed seminary? For Orthodox Judaism tradition has its origin in God as much as does the written word. Everything in the Talmud has the same value and the same origin as the words of the Bible . . .
4. What will rabbinic law and custom mean in the proposed seminary? Orthodox Judaism teaches that it is a divine obligation never to depart from the law and even customs carry the same obligation as vows. (Samson Raphael Hirsch, questions addressed to Zacharias Frankel)

Hirsch himself had had an excellent secular education and believed that it was possible to be an observant Jew while being fully conversant with modern culture. Nonetheless, he believed that there could be no compromise with the Reformers:

For them [the Reform], religion is only valid as long as it in no way impedes secular progress. For us [the Orthodox] progress is only valid as long as it in no way impedes religion . . . We declare before Heaven and earth that if our religion so commanded us we would abandon so-called civilization and progress. We would obey without question because we believe that our religion is true religion. It is the word of God and before it every other consideration must yield . . . The Jew has to judge everything by the unchangeable touchstone of his God-given law. Anything which does not pass this test does not exist for him. (Samson Raphael Hirsch, essays in *Jeschurun*).

In 1886, in the United States, it was decided to set up a more conservative seminary as a counterweight to the Hebrew Union College. This became the Jewish Theological Seminary of New York:

The American Hebrew supported the Union and the Union College, until all hope of having Judaism taught in the College and in the lives of the preceptors became demonstrably vain. We have had to become reconciled to the necessity of starting a new institution free from the shadow of the baneful influences which have perverted the Cincinnati institution. We may say this out of hostility to no man, but out of love for the ancestral faith which the head of the Cincinnati College and his followers seem in league to destroy. (Article in the *American Hebrew*, 1886)

Suggested Further Reading

A. Geiger, *Judaism and its History*, trans. M. Mayer, New York, 1866.

S. R. Hirsch, *The Nineteen Letters on Judaism*, Spring Valley, NY: Philipp Feldheim, 1994.

M. Mendelssohn, *Jerusalem and Other Jewish Writings*, trans. A. Jospe, New York: Schocken Books, 1969.

The Union Prayer Book of the Central Conference of American Rabbis, New York: CCAR Press, 1894.

Chronological Table

Circa CE	Documents	Events in Jewish History
1650–1700	Spinoza's *Tractatus*	Golden Age of Dutch Jewry
1750–1800	Dohm's *Amelioration*; Joseph II's edict; Mendelssohn's *Alim* and *Jerusalem*	Beginning of Haskalah
1800–1850	Assembly records; Frank's sermon; Harby's lecture; Hamburg Temple constitution; Heine's *Germany*; Geiger's *Journal*; Jacobson's Dedication; *Journal of the Science of Judaism*; *These Are the Words*; Trier's *Rabbinic Opinions*; Wechsler's *Rabbinic Opinions*	Spread of Haskalah Founding of first Reform Temples in Western Europe and USA
1850–1900	*American Hebrew* article; Gottlober's *Memoirs;* Hirsch's *Questions and Essays*; Mendes protest; Pittsburgh Platform; Wise's Appeal; Union Prayer Book	Founding of US rabbinical seminary Founding of Neo-Orthodox institutions in Europe and the US

11

Anti-Semitism and Zionism

1. The Rise of Anti-Semitism

The term 'anti-Semitism' was first used by the journalist Wilhelm Marr in the 1870s. In his *Victory of Judaism over Germanism*, he argued that German civilization was being destroyed by the Jews:

> They [the Jews] should not be blamed for this. For 1800 years they have battled against the Western world and they have defeated it and subjugated it. We are the losers in this battle and it is natural that the victors should proclaim 'Vae victis!' We have become so Judaised that we are outside salvation and a brutal anti-Semitic outburst will merely postpone the collapse of our Judaised society. It will not prevent it. The great mission of Judaisation is unstoppable . . . I am writing on behalf of an unhappy and enslaved people. These people are crying out under your [the Jews'] yoke just as you have cried out under ours, but which eventually you have put round our neck. The twilight of the gods has begun. You are the masters and we are the slaves. It is the end of Germany.

By the 1870s and 1880s anti-Semitism had become fashionable in Germany:

> Members of the Jewish tribe do not work. They exploit the mental or manual work of others. This alien tribe has enslaved the people of Germany. Basically the social question is the Jewish question. Everything else is fraud. (Otto Glagau, article in *Die Gartenlaube*)

> The Jews are our misfortune. (Heinrich Treitschke, article in *Preussische Jahrbücher*)

Anti-Semitism was also prevalent in France. It was the Dreyfus case of 1894 which brought the issue into the national forum:

> There are forty thousand military officers in France. Captain Dreyfus is

merely one of this forty thousand . . . If he had been a Catholic or a free-thinker, he would have been classified as an isolated extraordinary case, which recur throughout history. The next day the public would have been interested in other matters . . . However, now everybody in France is speaking of only one man and of his treason and that is because that man is a Jew. (Emmanuel Bucheron, article in *Le Figaro*)

I became a Zionist because of the Dreyfus trial, which I attended in 1894 . . . The wild screams of the street mob near the building of the military school where it was ordered that Dreyfus be deprived of his rank still resounds in my ears. (Theodor Herzl, *The Jewish State*)

In 1897, the real traitor was identified. In January 1898 the novelist Emil Zola addressed an open letter to the president of the Republic:

These, Monsieur le President, are the facts. This is how the judicial error can be explained. The moral proofs, the position of Dreyfus as a wealthy man, the absence of motive, the continual cry of innocence, complete the demonstration that Dreyfus is a victim of the extraordinary fantasies of Major du Paty de Clam, of his clerical surroundings and of the victimization of the 'filthy Jews', which is a disgrace to our era. (Emil Zola, 'J'accuse' in *L'Aurore*)

During this period the *Protocols of the Elders of Zion* was drafted. This forgery was supposedly written by a group of powerful Jews who were conspiring to take over the world. It has been reprinted many times and is currently enjoying a revival in the Arab world and in the newly independent states of the old Soviet Union:

When the times comes for our Ruler of the World to be crowned, we will see to it that by the same means – that is to say, by making use of the mob – we will destroy everything that may prove an obstacle in our way . . . We will create a universal economic crisis by all possible underhand means and with the help of gold, which is all in our hands . . . We have set at variance with one another all personal and national interests of the gentiles by promulgating religious and tribal prejudices among them for nearly twenty centuries. To all this, the fact is due that not one single government will find support from its neighbours when it calls upon them for it, in opposing us, because each one of them will think that action against us might be disastrous for its individual existence. We are too powerful – the world has to reckon with us. Governments cannot make even a small treaty without our being secretly involved in it.

In Russia anti-Semitism became official state policy:

The principal restrictions imposed on the Jews in Russia have frequently been described, but it may be useful briefly to recapitulate them:

With the exception of merchants of the first guild . . . students . . . apothecaries, dentists, surgeons and midwives, retired soldiers . . . and duly qualified artisans, no Jews are allowed to reside outside Poland and the fifteen governments which constitute the Jewish Pale . . .

Jews, with the exception of army doctors, are not allowed to hold any government appointment . . .

Every possible difficulty is placed in the way of Jews entering the schools and universities by the introduction of a percentage system . . .

Before a Jew can become a fully qualified barrister or lawyer, the consent of the Minister of Justice must be obtained. For fifteen years the consent was never given . . .

No Jew may elect or be elected a member of a Duma or municipal council, even in towns where they form eighty per cent of the total population. . . .

The Jews must pay a special meat tax on meat killed after the Jewish rite. (Charles Hardinge, *Journey to Some of the Principal Towns of Western and Southern Russia*)

2. Pogroms and Emigration

Pogroms against the Jews were common in Russia between 1881 and 1921:

The rumour got around that the Czar had authorized three days for the pillaging of Jewish property. In many places the rumour seemed to be confirmed by the negligence of the police, the casual attitude of officials and even the passivity of the soldiery who watched the looting of the Jews' houses with their guns under their arms. Jews who tried to defend themselves were arrested and disarmed. Others who were brave enough to stand guard in front of their houses with guns in their hands were threatened. (Anatole Leroy-Beaulieu, *L'Empire des Tsars et les Russes*)

Relations between the Jews and the Russian peasants were perpetually uneasy:

When Easter approached or when it was Christmas Eve, when the parish priest had inflamed the peasants' imaginations, after the long processions had wound their way around the town and passed the doors of the liquor shop, the excited peasants worked through their piety and hostility in government liquor. The Jewish households were seized by terror. Schoolboys used to tell the tale that Reuvele the coachman used to keep an iron rod in the leg of his boot on those days – in case of trouble . . .

Then came the days of the first revolution and the Black Hundreds were organized. Then there was the massacre at Kishinev and the pogroms in Homel. Dark clouds were descending over the whole region of Stolpce. From 9 January 1905 there was a continual wave of agitation against the Jews. The newspapers were full of stories about the pogroms. Suspicious characters turned up in town. They were not there to buy or to sell, but they hung about with the peasants, stirring them up. When the peasants came out of church they were very agitated. Nice friendly peasants told us that inciters had come to the villages and that the date and the hour of the pogrom had been set. (Schneur Zalman Shazar, *Shtern Fartog: Zikhroynes, Dertsey Lungen*)

The pogrom at Kishinev is well documented. The peasants were stirred up by a pamphlet signed by a 'true Christian Workers' Party':

Brothers, in the name of Our Lord who shed his blood for us and in the name of our holy Czar who is filled with compassion for his people, let us cry out during our great holiday, 'Down with the Yids!' Down with these horrible vermin, these vampires slavering for the blood of Russians. Remember that in the Odessa pogrom, the soldiers helped the people. They will do it again because at least our Christian army is not yet overrun by Jews. Come and help us! Attack the filthy Yids! (Pamphlet distributed at Kishinev in 1903)

Forty-nine people were killed in the pogrom, five hundred were wounded and nearly one third of the houses were destroyed:

Bits of furniture, glass samovars and twisted lamps, fragments of linen and clothing, and ripped mattresses and pillows were scattered everywhere. The streets looked as if there had been a snowstorm. They were covered with feathers as were the trees. (Report of the Judicial Committee on the Kishinev Pogrom)

The early twentieth century was a time of revolutionary fervour in Russia; many educated Jews were involved in the agitation:

The Jewish socialist intelligentsia abandoned the mass of Jewish people and left them to the natural course of events. The natural course of events meant pogroms which hurt the poor most. The appalling scenes of chaos and the atrocities inflicted upon tens of thousands of Jewish families and, following that, the cynical anti-Semitic propaganda put out by many Russian newspapers . . . opened the eyes of the Jewish socialist intelligentsia. They saw their mistakes and the ills to which they had subjected the Jewish poor and this at last aroused their compassion and anxiety. (Pavel Borisovich Axelrod, Pamphlet XXIX)

For many the only solution was emigration:

> Almost as far as my memory goes back, I can remember the stampede –
> the frantic rush from the Russian prison house; the tremendous tide of
> migration which carried hundreds of thousands of Jews from their ancient
> homes to far-off lands across the seas. I was a witness in boyhood and early
> manhood of the emptying of whole villages and towns. My own family was
> once caught up in the fever – this was about the time of the Kishinev
> pogrom of 1903 and though we finally decided against flight, there were
> cousins and uncles and more distant relatives by the score who took the
> westward path. (Chaim Weizmann, *Trial and Error: The Autobiography of
> Chaim Weizmann*)

Conditions on the voyage to the United States were miserable:

> Crowds everywhere, ill-smelling bunks, uninviting washrooms – this is
> steerage. The odours of scattered orange peelings, tobacco, garlic and dis-
> infectants meeting, but not blending. No lounge or chairs for comfort, and
> a continual babel of tongues – this is steerage. The food, which is miserable,
> is dealt out of huge kettles into the dinner pails provided by the steamship
> company. When it is distributed, the stronger push and crowd. (Edward
> Steiner, *On the Trail of the Immigrant*)

In 1892 the Hebrew Immigrant Aid Society (HIAS) was founded to help
the new immigrants as they settled in the United States:

> The immigrants who have been admitted, but have neither relatives nor
> friends to receive them, are taken by these same agents to the office of
> the HIAS . . . They will be accompanied together with their baggage,
> either to their respective destinations in other parts of the city, or to the
> railway station to continue their journey. The agents who undertake this
> duty are entirely worthy of confidence, and their services are rendered
> without any charge whatever . . . The home of the HIAS is open day
> and night . . . Accommodations are provided for men, women and chil-
> dren . . . Pen, ink and paper are supplied free, as are also newspapers.
> Immigrants may use this society as a forwarding address for letters.
> There are excellent baths, always at the free disposal of guests. (Bulletin
> for New Immigrants, Connecticut Daughters of the American
> Revolution)

Between 1840 and 1925, 2,713,000 Jewish immigrants entered the United
States and 391,000 settled elsewhere in the world. Stories of the hard-
ships of emigration are still circulated in families:

> My parents were from Poland. Right after World War I my father decided

he wanted to leave because he didn't see any future in Europe. He and my mother were married and then immediately after the wedding he went to the United States. My mother stayed at home waiting for him to be able to bring her over. They didn't see each other for eight years. So when this boatload of immigrants were waiting to get off the boat, my father recognized my mother, but she didn't recognize him. She said, 'You're not my husband!' When my father had left he was a thin man and he had put on a lot of weight in the eight years. So she said, 'Take off your coat.' She thought maybe his clothes were bulky, but she still didn't recognize him. Then she said, 'Take off your hat,' because he had a beautiful head of red hair when he left. Well he'd lost all his hair and when he took off his hat he was almost bald. So she said to him, 'Take off your glasses.' He hadn't worn glasses when he left, but when he took his glasses off she still did not recognize him. All the people standing by were hysterical with laughter and one of the group yelled out, 'Tell him to take off his pants!' (Lavinia and Dan Cohn-Sherbok, *The American Jew*)

3. Theodor Herzl and the Zionist Dream

The dream of returning to the Promised Land has been retained throughout Jewish history and is expressed in the liturgy:

This is the bread of affliction which our forefathers ate in the land of Egypt. Let all who are hungry come and eat. Let all who are needy come and celebrate the Passover. This year we are here; next year we will be in the Land of Israel. This year we are slaves; next year we will be free . . . O build Jerusalem, the holy city, speedily in our days. Blessed art thou, O God, who in his mercy builds Jerusalem . . . Blessed art thou, O Lord our God, King of the Universe, who brings forth the vine and its fruits; who brings forth produce of the fields and the pleasures of the land, which is the inheritance of our fathers to love and to enjoy. Pour out thy compassion, O God, on thy people Israel and build Jerusalem, the holy city, speedily in our own day . . . Next year in Jerusalem! (From the traditional Passover service)

After the Russian pogroms, several thousand Jews left for Palestine:

The recent pogroms have shaken the complacent Jews from their happy unconsciousness. Until now I was not interested in my origins. I saw myself as a good son of Russia, which was my justification – indeed the very air I breathed. I took enormous pride in every new discovery by a Russian scientist, every serious literary work, every Russian victory. I wanted to devote myself completely to the good of Russia and to do my duty cheerfully. Then suddenly the Russians themselves come and show us the door. They openly announce that we are free to leave. (Hayyim Hisin, Diary)

We want to conquer Palestine and gain for the Jews the political independence which was lost two thousand years ago. This is not a fantasy. We must establish farms, factories and industry. The developed industry must be put in Jewish hands. Most important of all, the young people must receive military training and be issued with proper weapons. Then the glorious day will come, as prophesied by Isaiah, when Israel will be restored. With their weapons in their hands, the Jews will declare that they are rulers of their ancient native land. (Zeev Dubnow, letter to his brother)

At the same time that the first pioneers were leaving for Palestine, Leon Pinsker argued in his pamphlet 'Auto-emancipation' that Jewish freedom could only be secured by the establishment of a Jewish political state:

For the living the Jew is a dead man; for the natives of a country the Jew is a foreigner and a vagrant; for those who own property he is a beggar; for the poor, he is a millionaire and their exploiter; for patriots he is a man without a country and for people of every class he is a hated rival.

The founder of political Zionism was Theodor Herzl, who convened the First Zionist Conference in Basle in 1897 and who was the author of *The Jewish State*:

The whole plan is fundamentally simple, as indeed it must be if everyone is to understand it. Let sovereignty be granted us over a sufficient portion of the world so that our rightful national requirements are met. We ourselves will manage everything else. It is neither ridiculous nor impossible to create a new sovereign state. As we have seen, it has happened in our own time among people who were not mainly middle-class, as we are, but among those who were poorer, less educated and weaker than ourselves. Those governments whose countries are plagued by anti-Semitism will be very interested in procuring this sovereignty for us . . .

The Jews will not leave for their new country all at once. It will be a gradual exodus lasting several decades. First the poorest will go and they will bring the land under cultivation. Following a set plan, they will construct roads, bridges and railways. They will establish telecommunications; they will divert rivers and will build themselves homes. Their labour will create trade. Trade will create markets and markets will attract new settlers . . . The labour invested in agriculture will give new value to the land and other Jews will soon see that a new and permanent opportunity has opened for them. They will be able to use their own enterprise which in the past has only earned them hatred and execration.

Herzl was willing to consider other places besides Palestine for a Jewish homeland:

Which should be preferred? Palestine or the Argentine? The Society will accept which ever is given and whatever the Jewish public prefers. (Ibid.)

In 1903, after the Kishinev pogrom (see this chapter, Part 2), the British were willing to offer a portion of Uganda:

Lord Landsdowne will be prepared to entertain favourably proposals for the establishment of a Jewish colony or settlement on conditions which will enable the members to observe their national customs. For this purpose, he will be prepared to discuss (if a suitable site has been found and subject to the views of the advisors to the Secretary of State of East Africa) the details of a scheme. (Sir Clement Hill, negotiations for a Jewish colony in Uganda, 1903)

This proposal was sharply criticized at the Sixth Zionist Conference. Herzl himself died in 1904 and was buried in Vienna and would remain buried there 'until the day when the Jewish people transfer my remains to Palestine'.

4. The Zionist Movement

A second wave of immigrants departed for the Promised Lane in 1904. Among them was Aharon David Gordon. He believed that manual labour was essential for the salvation of the Jewish people:

A people that was completely divorced from nature, that during two thousand years was imprisoned within walls, that became inured to all forms of life except to a life of labour, cannot become once again a living, natural, working people without bending all its willpower towards that end. We lack the fundamental element: we lack labour (not labour done because of necessity, but labour to which man is naturally and organically linked), labour by which a people becomes rooted in its soil and its culture. (Aharon David Gordon, *Labour*)

From the earliest days there was a determination to create a Hebrew rather than a Yiddish culture. Asher Zvi Ginsberg (later known as Ahad Ha-Am) argued that it was impossible for Eastern European Jewry to return to the traditional religious symbolism of the ghetto; instead a new Jewish social identity must be established:

> Judaism needs but little at present. It does not need an independent state, but it must create in its native land the conditions that will favour its development. It needs a good-sized settlement of Jews working without hindrance in every branch of culture, from agriculture to handicrafts, from science to literature. This Jewish settlement, which will be a gradual growth, will, in the course of time, become the focal point of the nation, in which its spirit will find pure expression and in all its aspects develop to the highest pitch of perfection of which it is capable. Then, from the centre, the spirit of Judaism will go out to the huge circumference, to all the communities of the Dispersion. It will breathe new life into them and preserve their unity. And when our national culture in Palestine has reached this level, we can be sure that it will produce men in the country who will be capable, with a favourable opportunity, of establishing a state that will be a real Jewish state, not merely a state of the Jews. (Ahad Ha-Am, *The Jewish State and the Jewish Problem*)

Ahad Ha-Am realized that there would be difficulties in the future with the Arab population of Palestine:

> We tend to believe that nowadays Palestine is almost completely deserted, that it is an uncultivated desert and that anyone can go there and buy as much land as he wants. In fact this is not the case. In the country it is difficult to find anywhere Arab land which lies fallow . . . When the day comes in which the life of our people in the land of Israel will develop to such a degree, the local population will be pushed aside by little or much. Then the local Arabs will not easily give up their place. (Ahad Ha-Am, *Truth from the Land of Israel*)

From the earliest days of Zionism there were different parties within the movement. Some early writers tried to justify a return to Zion on religious grounds:

> When Jews who are pious and learned in Jewish law willingly go to the Land of Israel and make their homes in Jerusalem; when they are motivated by a desire to serve, by a purity of spirit and by a love of holiness; when they come by ones and twos from all the four corners of the earth; when many have settled there and their prayer increased at the holy mountain in Jerusalem, then the Creator will take notice and he will hasten the day of our redemption. (Zvi Hirsch Kalischer, *Seeking Zion*)

However, Herzl's World Zionist Organization was essentially secular in orientation:

> Those Jews who want it will achieve their state. We will live as free men on
> our own soil at last and we will peacefully die in our own homes. The world
> will be liberated by our freedom. It will be enriched by our wealth. It will
> be magnified by our greatness. Whatever we attempt for our own benefit
> in our own land will rebound mightily and beneficially for the good of all
> humanity. (Theodor Herzl, *The Jewish State*)

After the Fifth Zionist Conference of 1901, the Mizrachi party, the religious wing of the Zionist movement, was formed:

> Mizrachi is an organization of Zionists who follow the Basle programme and
> desire to work for the perpetuation of Jewish national life. Mizrachi sees the
> perpetuation of the Jewish people in the observance of Torah, Jewish tradi-
> tion and the mitzvot [commandments] and the return to the land of our fore-
> fathers. (Programme of the Mizrachi Movement, 1904)

Meanwhile, others insisted that the role of Zionism was to create a socialist state – a secularized version of the messianic vision:

> Proletarian Zionism is possible only if its aims can be achieved through
> the class struggle; Zionism can only be realized if proletarian Zionism is
> realized . . . The Jewish proletariat is in need of revolution more than any
> other. It is hoping most ardently for the good that is expected to come
> with the growth of democracy in society. The terrible national oppres-
> sion; the exploitation on the part of petty Jewish capitalists; and the com-
> paratively high cultural level and restlessness of the city-bred Jewish pro-
> letarian, the son of the 'People of the Book' – these generate an over-
> whelming revolutionary energy and an exalted spirit of self-sacrifice . . .
> Political territorial autonomy in Palestine is the ultimate aim of Zionism.
> For proletarian Zionists, this is also a step towards socialism. (Ber Borochov,
> *Our Platform*)

In 1912, Agudat Israel was formed which opposed any form of political
Zionism. It was identified with the ultra-Orthodox and one of their
spokesmen, Rabbi Joseph Sonnenfeld described the secular Zionists as
'evil men and ruffians'. At the other end of the religious spectrum,
Zionism was also rejected by many Reform Jews:

> We denounce the whole question of a Jewish state as foreign to the spirit of
> the modern Jew of this land, who looks upon America as his Palestine and
> whose interests are centred here. (Isaac Mayer Wise, speaking at the First
> Zionist Conference)

5. The Impact of World War I on the Jewish Community

According to the demographer Jacob Lestschinsky the distribution of Jews around the world between 1850 and 1939 was as follows:

	1880	1914	1939
	M i l l i o n s		
Whole World (Continents)	7.7	13.5	16.6
Europe			
E. Europe	5.4	7.1	7.5
W. Europe	1.4	2.0	2.0
Asia			
Palestine	0.0	0.1	0.4
Other	0.3	0.4	0.6
Africa	0.3	0.4	0.6
USA/Australia	0.3	3.5	5.5

(Based on J. Lestschinsky, *Crisis, Catastrophe and Survival*)

Jews fought for their countries on both sides in World War I:

> Our dear country, our beloved Russia, has been challenged to a bloody and dangerous duel. It is an uncompromising struggle for the greatness and integrity of Russia. All the true sons of the fatherland have stood up like a single man to offer their breasts as a defence against the common enemy. Everywhere in the Russian empire, the Jews, our religious brothers, are eagerly doing their duty. Many have offered themselves as volunteers. (Editorial of *Novy Voskhod*, a Lithuanian Jewish newspaper)

During the war, the British government showed its sympathy with the Zionist movement in the Balfour Declaration of 1917. It was hoped that an appeal to Zionist sentiment would encourage Russian Jews to continue to support the Allies and prevent revolutionary Russian from abandoning the war effort:

His Majesty's Government views with favour the establishment in Palestine of a national home for the Jewish people, and will use their best endeavours to facilitate the achievement of this object, it being clearly understood that nothing shall be done which may prejudice the civil and religious rights of the existing non-Jewish communities in Palestine, or the rights and political status enjoyed by Jews in any other country. (Arthur Balfour, letter to Lord Rothschild)

The Russian Revolution, however, unleashed still further the forces of anti-Semitism:

Awake, you people of Russia. Take your club. Let us expel the Jewish villains who are despoiling Russia. In Germany, in all of Poland, Galicia, Kiev, Berditshev, these scoundrels are hunted down and thrown out. You alone in your simple stupidity, continue to obey the orders of Trotsky, Nakhamkess, Zederbaum and all the rest. (Proclamation to the Red Army, 1919)

After the Revolution, various solutions were offered to the 'Jewish Problem'. In 1934, the Soviet Government declared Birobidzhan to be a Jewish Autonomous Region and open for Jewish settlement:

Within a decade, Birobidzhan will be the most important and probably the only bulwark of national Jewish socialist culture . . . The transformation of the region into a republic is only a question of time. (Mikhail Kalinin in a speech to the representatives of Moscow workers and the Yiddish press)

Even the upward mobility and social success of the Jewish immigrants in the United States was regarded with suspicion by some of the more conservative Christian Americans:

Down in a tall busy street he read a dozen Jewish names on a line of stores. In the door of each store stood a dark little man watching the passers-by with intent eyes, eyes gleaming with suspicion, with pride, with clarity, with cupidity, with comprehension. New York – he could not disassociate it now from the slow upward creep of this people. The little stores, growing, expanding, consolidating, moving, watched over with hawks' eyes and a bee's attention to detail. They slithered out on all sides. It was impressive. In perspective it was tremendous. (F. Scott Fitzgerald, *The Beautiful and the Damned*)

By the 1930s, despite the Balfour declaration and the increasingly desperate situation in Europe, the British were limiting Jewish immigration to Palestine. Chaim Weizmann, who had become President of the World Zionist Organization, was trying to co-operate with the British:

I say to the Mandatory Power: You shall not outrage the Jewish nation. You shall not play fast and loose with the Jewish people. Say to us frankly that the National Home is closed and we shall know where we stand. But this trifling with a nation bleeding from a thousand wounds must not be done by the British whose Empire is built on moral principals — that mighty Empire must not commit this sin against the People of the Book. Tell us the truth. That at least we have deserved . . .

Further remember that England, although beset by anxious cares, has yet been the only power which has made a serious attempt to contribute to a solution of the Jewish problem. The present difficulties must not for a moment blind us to this fact. (Chaim Weizmann, evidence given before the Peel Committee, 1937)

Meanwhile, a significant minority, led by Vladimir Jabotinski, had formed a new Union of Zionist Revisionists who would accept no compromises:

I am going to make a terrible confession. Our demand for a Jewish majority is not our maximum — it is our minimum; it is just an inevitable stage if we are allowed to go on salvaging our people. The point where Jews will reach a majority in that country will not be the point of saturation yet — because with a million more Jews in Palestine today you would already have a Jewish majority. But there are certainly three or four million in the east who are virtually knocking at the door asking for admission . . .

Remember we have children and wives; legalize our self-defence as you are doing in Kenya. In Kenya until recently every European was obliged to train for the Settlers' Defence Force. Why should the Jews in Palestine be forced to prepare for self-defence underhand, as though committing a legal offence? . . . The Jews have never been allowed to prepare for the holy duty of self-defence, as every Englishman would have done. (Vladimir Jabotinski, evidence before the Peel Commission, 1937)

Suggested Further Reading

P. Dreyfus, ed., *Dreyfus: His Life and Letters*, London: Hutchinson, 1937.

T. Herzl, *The Jewish State*, trans. Sylvie d'Avigdor, London: Constable, 1955.

C. Weizmann, *Trial & Error: The Autobiography of Chaim Weizmann*, Westport, CT: Greenwood Press, 1972.

The Protocols of the Elders of Zion (many editions and translations)

Chronological Table

Circa BCE	Documents	Events in Jewish History
1860–80	Marr's *Victory*; Glagau's article; Treitschke's article; Kalischer's *Seeking Zion*	
1880–1900	Bacheron's article; Herzl's *Jewish State*; Zola's 'J'accuse'; *Protocols of the Elders of Zion*; Leroy-Beaulieu's *L'Empire*; Dubnow's letter; Pinsker's *Auto-emancipation*; Ha-Am's *Jewish State, Truth*; Wise's speech	Pogroms begin in Russia Dreyfus case Mass emigration to the US First Zionist Conference
1900–20	Hardinge's *Journey*; Kishinev pamphlet and report; Steiner's *Trail*; HIAS bulletin; Hill's negotiations; Gordon's *Labour*; Mizrachi programme; Borochov's *Platform*; *Novy Voskhod* editorial; Balfour declaration; Red Army proclamation	Pogroms in Russia Mass emigration from Eastern Europe Gradual Jewish settlement in Palestine
1920–40	Axelrod's pamphlet; Hisin's *Diary*; Kalinin's speech; Fitzgerald's *The Beautiful and The Damned*; Weizmann and Jabotinski's evidence to the Peel Commission	Emigration restrictions to Palestine, Western Europe and the United States Rise of Nazism
1940–60	Shazar's *Shtern Fartog*; Weizmann's *Autobiography*; Lestschinsky's *Crisis*	Holocaust of European Jewry Creation of the State of Israel

12

The Holocaust and its Aftermath

1. Nazi Anti-Semitism

The Nazi party in Germany achieved its spectacular success in the 1930s against a background of mass employment, weak government and economic crisis. From the start its leader Adolf Hitler was openly anti-Semitic:

> The part the Jews played in the social phenomenon of prostitution and, more particularly, in the traffic of white slaves could be studied better here [Vienna] than in any other Western European city . . . A cold shudder ran down my spine when I first realized that it was the same sort of cold-blooded, shameless, thick-skinned Jew who showed his consummate skill in conducting that disgusting exploitation of the dregs of the big city. (Adolf Hitler, *Mein Kampf*)

Hitler argued that the Jew undermined the racial purity of the German people:

> The black-haired Jewish youth lies in wait for hours on end, satanically glaring at and spying on the unsuspicious girl whom he plans to seduce, adulterating her blood and removing her from the bosom of her own people. The Jew uses every possible means to undermine the racial foundations of a subjugated people. In his systematic efforts to ruin women and girls, he strives to break down the final barriers of discrimination between him and other peoples. The Jews were responsible for bringing Negroes into the Rhineland, with the ultimate intention of bastardizing the white race which they hate and thus lowering its cultural and political level so that the Jew might dominate. For as long as a people remain racially pure and are conscious of the treasure of their blood, they can never be conquered by the Jew. Never in this world can the Jew become the master of any people except a bastardized people. (Ibid.)

From the start Hitler made his intentions clear:

At the start of the war, or even during the course of it, if twelve or fifteen thousand of these Jews who were corrupting the nation had been forced to submit to poison gas, just as hundreds of thousands of our best German workers from every social stratum and from every trade and calling had to face it in the field, then the millions of sacrifices made at the front would not have been in vain. (Ibid.)

Hitler became Chancellor of Germany in 1933 and in 1935 the Nuremberg Laws were passed:

A citizen of the Reich is only that subject who is of German or cognate blood and who, through his conduct, shows that he is both desirous and fit to serve faithfully the German people and the Reich.

Marriages between Jews and citizens of German or cognate blood are forbidden; extra-marital relations between Jews and citizens of German and cognate blood are forbidden: Jews may not employ female citizens of German and cognate blood under forty-five years in their households; Jews are forbidden to hoist the Reich and national flag and to display the colours of the Reich. The display of Jewish colours is permissible under state protection.

In 1938, the German army invaded Austria. The Nazis set themselves the task of publicly humiliating the Jewish population:

The SS sentries threw out the Chief Rabbi, Dr Taglicht, a man of seventy, and he, like myself, was ordered to brush these pavements. In order that he should feel the full force of the degradation and the humility of it, he was thrown out wearing his gown and with his prayer shawl on. (Reminiscence of Moritz Fleischmann collected in Martin Gilbert, *The Holocaust*)

On the night of 9 November 1938, attacks on Jews, synagogues and Jewish property were made throughout Germany and Austria:

On the evening of 9 November 1938, the Reich propaganda minister, party comrade Dr Goebbels, informed the party leaders who had gathered for an evening of comradeship in the Old Town Hall in Munich that there had been anti-Jewish demonstrations in the district of Kurhess and Magdeburg-Anhalt; several synagogues had been set alight and Jewish businesses destroyed. At his [Goebbels'] suggestion, the Fuhrer had decided that such demonstrations were neither to be prepared nor organized by the party, but insofar as they were spontaneous in origin, they should likewise not be quelled . . . These instructions, with this understanding, were passed on immediately . . . by a large number of party members in attendance at the party headquarters of their respective party districts over the telephone. (Report of the Supreme Party Tribunal, 1939)

The events of Kristallnacht, as it came to be called, were reported with extraordinary cynicism in the Nazi press:

> All over the west side of Berlin, as in other parts of the capital where Jews still strut and swagger, not a single store-front window of a Jewish business has remained intact . . . The three Berlin synagogues were set ablaze . . . In all of Berlin's streets, in the towns of Mark Brandenburg, everywhere where Jews live and 'work', passers-by are greeted with the same vista – a gaping void in the emptied display cases and store windows and not a Jew to be seen anywhere . . . people only acknowledge the demolished store windows in passing, although not without a quite understandable sense of delight and satisfaction at the sight. (Report in *Volkischer Beobachter*, 11 November 1938)

Many Jews tried to escape abroad, but it was very hard to obtain an immigration visa:

> I came from a German household in Berlin where we only went to the Temple on High Holy Days. It was a very musical household with my father listening to Bach concertos . . . It was an intellectual household and a well-to-do household. My father had a very successful welding company with about a hundred employees. I was born in 1921 and the Nazis came to power when I was eleven years old. Interestingly enough, whatever the Nazis did, they did in the smaller communities rather than in a big metropolis like Berlin. I only really knew what the Nazis were up to when we had to turn in all our silver and gold. That was sometime in 1937. Then came Kristallnacht. We did not live in the area where all the Jewish stores were and where the famous synagogue was, but my mother took me by underground to see it. So I have a very vivid picture of all the broken glass, the smoke of burning buildings and total destruction. That was the first time my parents really said, 'Our child has to get out of Germany.' I had cousins in America, but my immigration quota number hadn't been called so I left Germany for England on a domestic permit. My piano teacher arranged for me to work domestically with a family, and that's how I got out with ten dollars in my pocket. You couldn't take out more than that . . . I was still in contact with my parents until 1941. Then all stopped and I knew they had been taken away. (Lavinia and Dan Cohn-Sherbok, *The American Jew*)

2. The Final Solution

Once the Nazis had invaded Poland in September 1939 escape by emigration was impossible. Poland had a very large Jewish population who were put to work for the regime. This was described by the Nazi leaders as 'destruction by work':

The forced labour decree gnaws away at our people. Because of the extent of the catastrophe, the Jews do not believe that it will come to pass. Even though they know the nature of the conqueror very very well and his tyrannical attitude towards them has already been felt on their backs; even though they know he has no pity or human feeling in relation to the Jews – in spite of all this, their attitude towards the terrible decree he has published is one of frivolity. I do not join them in this. Thousands and perhaps tens of thousands will become slave labourers. (Chaim Kaplan, *Scroll of Agony*)

After the invasion of Russia in 1941, special troops known as the Einsatzgruppen were employed to deal with the Jews:

[Jews] were placed alive in anti-tank trenches about two kilometres long and killed by machine guns. Lime was thereupon sprayed upon them and a second row of Jews was made to lie down. They were similarly shot . . . Only the children were not shot. They were caught by the legs, their heads hit against stones and they were thereupon buried alive. (Interrogation report of a liberated prisoner on Alderney in the Channel Islands, 1944)

Forced labour and random killing were not considered to be a sufficiently efficient method of dealing with the Jews. At the Wannsee Conference of 20 January 1942, the 'Final Solution of the European Jewish Question' was outlined and explained:

In the course of the final solution, the Jews should be brought under appropriate direction in a suitable manner to the East for labour utilization. Separated by sex, the Jews capable of work will be led into these areas in large labour columns to build roads, whereby doubtless a large part will fall away through natural reduction. The inevitable final remainder which doubtless constitutes the toughest elements will have to be dealt with appropriately, since it represents a natural selection which upon liberation is to be regarded as a germ cell of a new Jewish development . . .

 In the course of the practical implementation of the final solution, Europe will be combed from West to East . . . For the moment the evacuated Jews will be brought bit by bit to the so-called transit ghettos from where they will be transported further east. ('Protocol of the Wannsee Conference', document used by the International Military Tribunal, Nuremburg)

A network of concentration and extermination camps was set up. People were deported and either set to work on starvation rations or murdered immediately:

Passover 1944, the last day was the Sabbath; I studied the Talmud with my father. Next day the Hungarian gendarmes came and put the Jews in the ghetto. We were there maybe two or three weeks. Then we were put on the cattle trains in the usual way to Auschwitz. We went for two days and two nights. It was my father, my mother, myself and two of my sisters. We arrived after a long suffering trip, with no facilities in a cattle car. We came at night. With the lights we couldn't do anything. A minute and I was here; my father was there; my mother was there; my sisters were some place else. We got separated so fast. No one could even say a word. So I suspect my parents were gassed the same night . . .

I was in Auschwitz probably two weeks or so, and then I was taken to Mathausen. Two thousand of us, young people. We arrived on Shavuot. The reason? They were building about twenty-eight tunnels into the mountains to hide airplane factories. They needed labour very badly. We were put to work there, but the reception committee, so to speak, made us stand to attention for almost four hours in the sun just to humiliate us. The assessor came afterwards with a whip and a dog to look at us and yell, 'Yuden, look at the chimney over there. That's the only place you can get out of here.' That was the reception. (Lavinia and Dan Cohn-Sherbok, *The American Jew*)

The whole operation was conducted with ruthless efficiency. However there were pockets of resistance. In April 1943, the Warsaw ghetto erupted:

All of a sudden they started entering the ghetto, thousands armed as if they were going to the front against Russia. And we, some twenty men and women, young. And what were our arms? The arms we had – we had a revolver, a grenade and a whole group had two guns, and some bombs, home-made, prepared in a very primitive way. We had to light it using matches and Molotov bottles. It was very strange to see those twenty men and women, standing up against the armed great enemy, glad and merry, because we knew that their end will come . . . When the Germans came up to our posts and marched by we threw those hand grenades and bombs and saw German blood pouring over the streets of Warsaw and, because we had seen so much Jewish blood running in the streets of Warsaw before that, there was rejoicing . . . And after an hour we saw the officer hastening his soldiers to retreat, to collect their dead and their wounded. But they did not move, they did not collect their dead and their wounded. We took their arms later. And thus on the first day, we the few with our poor arms drove the Germans away from the ghetto. (Testimony of Zivia Lubetkin at the Eichmann Trial 1961 in Martin Gilbert, *The Holocaust*)

By the end of World War II in 1945, European Jewry was decimated. The old synagogues, communities and places of Jewish learning were gone for ever:

Warsaw, 28 April 1943, death can wait no longer. From the floors above me the firing becomes weaker by the minute. The last defenders of this strong-hold are now falling, and with them falls and perishes the great, beautiful and God-fearing Jewish part of Warsaw. The sun is about to set, and I thank God that I will never see it again. Fire lights my small window, and the bit of sun that I can see is flooded with red like a waterfall of blood. In about an hour at the most I will be with the rest of my family and with the mil-lions of other stricken members of my people in that better world where there are no more questions. (Zvi Kolitz, *Yossel Rakover's Appeal to God*)

3. The Creation of the State of Israel

The Peel Commission of 1937 had proposed to partition Palestine into a Jewish and an Arab state. The Jewish portion was to include the fol-lowing:

> Starting from Ras al-Naqura it follows the existing northern and eastern frontier of Palestine to Lake Tiberias and crosses the lake to the outflow of the River Jordan whence it continues down the river to a point a little north of Beisan. It then cuts across the Beisan Plain and runs along the southern edge of the valley of Jezreel and across the plain of Jezreel to a point near Megiddo, whence it crosses the Carmel ridge in the neighbourhood of the Megiddo road. Having thus reached the Maritime Plain the line runs southward down its eastern edge until it reaches the Jerusalem-Joppa cor-ridor near Lydda. South of the corridor it continues down the edge of the plain to a point about ten miles south of Rehovot whence it turns west to the sea.

The partition plan was abandoned in the 1939 White Paper. During World War II the British did their best to prevent illegal Jewish landings in Palestine despite the desperate situation of European Jewry. In 1942 the Biltmore Program was proposed and subsequently endorsed by all the major Jewish organizations of the United States:

> The new world order that will follow victory cannot be established on foun-dations of peace, justice and equality unless the problem of Jewish home-lessness is finally solved. The conference demands that the gates of Palestine be opened; that the Jewish Agency be vested with control of immigration into Palestine and with the necessary authority for the upbuilding of the country, including the development of uncultivated and unsettled areas; and that Palestine be established as a Jewish commonwealth integrated into the structure of the new democratic world. (Biltmore Program, 1942)

Relations between the British and the Jews were further impaired in 1944 by the murder of Lord Moyne, a British Minister of State, by the Stern

Gang, a Jewish underground group:

A shameful crime has shocked the world and affected none more strongly than those, like myself, who, in the past, have been consistent friends of the Jews and constant architects of their future. If our dreams for Zionism are to end in the smoke of assassins' pistols, and one labours for its future to produce only a new set of gangsters worthy of Nazi Germany, many like myself would have to reconsider the position we have maintained so consistently and so long in the past. (Prime Minister Winston Churchill speaking to the House of Commons, 1944)

After the war ended in 1945, the restrictions on Jewish immigration to Palestine remained in place. Terrorist tactics were employed to persuade the British to leave:

PART OF KING DAVID HOTEL WRECKED. 39 persons were last night stated to have been killed and 53 to be missing after the attack by Jewish terrorists on the British headquarters in Jerusalem at midday yesterday. (*The Times*, 23 July 1946)

In November 1947 the United Nations recommended that the British Mandate be terminated and that Palestine be partitioned into two independent states. Among the thirty-three member states supporting the motion were both the United States and the Soviet Union:

It would be unjust if we failed to take into account this aspiration of the Jews to a state of their own and denied them the right to realize it. The withholding of that right cannot be justified, particularly when we consider all that happened to them in the Second World War. (Andrei Gromyko, Soviet Foreign Minister, speaking to the United Nations General Assembly)

Despite Arab attacks, the Jews under David Ben-Gurion (1886–1973) consolidated their position and on 14 May 1948 the independence of the Jewish State in Palestine was declared:

Inside the auditorium, behind the dais, hung a huge photograph of Theodor Herzl. The Philharmonic Orchestra played *Hatikva* which had been made the new state's national anthem. Then I held in my hand the Declaration, which I read with a heart filled at once with trepidation and exultation. I tried to overcome my emotion and read the Declaration in a loud clear tone, as everybody rose to hear it. Rabbi Maimon, the doyen of us all, recited the blessing thanking the Almighty for 'sustaining us so that we have lived to see this day . . .' Everybody present signed. I announced the State of Israel was now in existence and the meeting was adjourned. In the streets the throngs sang and danced. (David Ben-Gurion, *Israel: The Years of Challenge*)

Conflict between the Jews and the Palestinian Arabs continued for much of 1949. It broke out again in 1954, in 1967 and in 1973. To this day there is the problem of the Palestinian refugees displaced from their homes by the new state. The following report was written by a Jewish observer and appeared in the Israeli periodical *Davar*:

> Ten thousand people live on one square kilometre. A third generation living in overcrowded conditions, filth, lack of elementary sanitary conditions and degrading poverty. Seventy per cent of males are simple day workers who depend on work from the black labour market in Jerusalem. The schools are on a very low level and the many curfews disrupt them. The military government is strict and pressures them in all possible ways . . . No building is allowed. Requests for additional land that exists in plenty near the camp is refused. (Dov Yermia, article in *Davar*, 28 January 1985)

Nonetheless, Israel has survived. In 1967 in the Six Day War, Jerusalem was captured by the Israeli forces. Despite international pressure, in 1980 it was proclaimed the capital of Israel:

> 1. Jerusalem whole and united is the capital of Israel.
> 2. Jerusalem is the seat of the President of the State, the Knesset, the Government and the Supreme Court.
> 3. The Holy Places shall be protected from desecration and any other offence and from anything likely to prejudice the freedom of access of the members of the different religions to the places sacred to them or their feelings with regard to those places. (Law enacted by the Knesset, 1980)

4. Jewish Thought after the Holocaust

How was it possible to believe in an all-loving God after the Holocaust? No consensus has emerged among Jewish theologians; Ignaz Maybaum has argued that the suffering of the Jews in the Holocaust was the suffering of God's faithful servant for the sake of humanity:

> The events of the years 1933–1945 seemed unparalleled in mankind's history. Many Jews were stunned into silence, some into the religious rebellion of Job. God has allowed to happen what has happened; where is God? . . . My mother died in Theresienstadt, my two sisters and other relatives died in Auschwitz. Can I bring myself to conceive of any kind of progress coming as a consequence of this third churban [disaster]? Exodus is progress. The remnant must remain the people believing in God, the Redeemer from

Egypt . . . We are the remnant and of this we must speak with the Hallelujah
of the redeemed at the Red Sea . . . Golgotha with Christianity absenting
itself became a place of skulls. Auschwitz is the pagan Golgotha of our time.
(Ignaz Maybaum, *The Face of God after Auschwitz*)

Emil Fackenheim argued that the Holocaust was an expression of God's
will that his chosen people must survive:

Jews are forbidden to hand Hitler posthumous victories. They are commanded to survive as Jews, lest the Jewish people perish. They are commanded to remember the victims of Auschwitz lest their memories perish.
They are forbidden to despair of man and his world, and to escape into either
cynicism or other worldliness, lest they cooperate in delivering the world
over to the forces of Auschwitz. Finally they are forbidden to despair of the
God of Israel, lest Judaism perish . . . A Jew may not respond to Hitler's
attempt to destroy Judaism by himself cooperating in its destruction. In
ancient times, the unthinkable Jewish sin was idolatry. Today it is to respond
to Hitler by doing his work. (Emil Fackenheim, *God's Presence in History:
Jewish Affirmations and Philosophical Reflections*)

In Fackenheim's view Jews should make their home in the land of Israel:

What a Jew by birth can do in our time is to recognize that just as one kind
of Jew – the Torah student – set the unifying standard for all Jews, so the
standard is set today by another kind – the oleh [immigrant]. Although thoroughly at home in the country of birth, the oleh makes aliyah [immigrates
to Israel] because of love. (Emil Fackenheim, 'On the Jewish People, Zionism
and Israel', *Forum*, 1983)

The Orthodox theologian, Eliezer Berkovits argued that there was no
rational explanation for the Holocaust, but that nonetheless the Jews must
cling to their belief in God:

He [God] created evil by creating the possibility for evil; he made peace by
creating the possibility for it. He had to create the possibility for evil, if he
was to create the possibility for its opposite, peace, goodness, love . . . God's
very mercy and forbearance, his very love for man, necessitates the abandonment of some men to a fate they may well experience as indifferent to
justice and human suffering . . . Because of the necessity for his absence,
there is the 'Hiding of the Face' and the suffering of the innocent; because
of the necessity of his presence, evil will not ultimately triumph; because of
it, there is hope for man. (Eliezer Berkovits, *Faith after the Holocaust*)

If the traditional Jewish belief in a loving providential God is to be
retained in the face of the Holocaust, the present author has argued that

the traditional Pharisaic belief in life after death (see Chapter 4, Part 4) must also be retained:

> Because of this shift of emphasis in Jewish thought, it is not surprising that Jewish Holocaust theologians have refrained from appealing to the traditional belief in other-worldly reward and punishment in formulating their responses to the horrors of the death camps. Yet without this belief, it is simply impossible to make sense of the world as the creation of an all-good, all-powerful God. Without eventual vindication of the righteous in Paradise, there is no way to sustain the belief in a providential God who watches over his chosen people. (Dan Cohn-Sherbok, *Holocaust Theology*)

Other theologians have given up the struggle. Richard Rubenstein has argued that the Nazi death camps are a decisive refutation of the belief in a loving providential deity:

> The agony of European Jewry cannot be likened to the testing of Job. To see any purpose in the death camps, the traditional believer is forced to regard the most demonic, anti-human explosion of all history as a meaningful expression of God's purposes. The idea is simply too obscene for me to accept . . . When I say we live in the time of the death of God, I mean that the thread uniting God and man, heaven and earth, has been broken. We stand in a cold, silent, unfeeling cosmos, unaided by any powerful power beyond our own resources. After Auschwitz, what else can a Jew say about God? (Richard Rubenstein, *After Auschwitz*)

Subsequently Rubenstein has modified his view and he later espoused a mystical theology, influenced by the Eastern religious traditions:

> Perhaps the best available metaphor for the concept of God as the Holy Nothingness is that God is the ocean and we are the waves. In some sense each wave has its moment in which it is distinguishable as a somewhat separate entity. Nevertheless no wave is entirely distinct from the ocean which is its substantial ground. (Richard Rubenstein and John K. Roth, *Approaches to Auschwitz*)

After the Holocaust some Jews have maintained their religious beliefs and some have not:

> I served in Belgium, France, Germany. I was with the troops that helped liberate Buchenwald . . . I have a picture of me standing next to a sign on the outside of Buchenwald. People on their way to work passed that sign and the sign said in German, 'No one is allowed in the crematorium.' That changed my life . . . After the war I taught at the Temple as a volunteer . . . and they didn't have much trouble convincing me to do it full-time . . . What

do I look back on with the greatest satisfaction? Well, four of my students have become rabbis.(Lavinia and Dan Cohn-Sherbok, *The American Jew*).

I'm not a religious person after being in Auschwitz. (Ibid.)

5. The Jewish Community after World War II

The Holocaust and the founding of the State of Israel completely changed the distribution of world Jewry:

	1939	1948	1967
		Millions	
World	16.6	11.5	13.5
Eastern Europe (not Soviet Union)	4.7	0.8	0.3
Soviet Union in Europe	2.8	1.8	2.0
Western Europe	2.0	1.1	1.2
Palestine/Israel	0.4	0.6	2.4
Asia/Other	0.6	0.7	0.5
Africa	0.6	0.7	0.2
America/Australia	5.5	5.8	6.9

(Based on J. Lestschinsky, *Crisis, Catastrophe and Survival*; and *Encyclopaedia Judaica*)

Many of the survivors of the concentration camps either had no wish to return to their old homes or found they were not welcome when they did:

ANTI JEWISH RIOTS IN POLAND. It is reported though not yet officially confirmed that 36 Jews including the Chairman of the local Jewish community, Dr Kahane, were killed during grave anti-Jewish riots at Kielce, 120 miles from Warsaw today. The riots, according to a statement of the local Governor, came after rumours that the Jews had killed 12 Christian children for ritual purposes. Crowds attacked the Jewish communal centre, breaking into offices where several were killed. Four policemen were also wounded and one officer killed. Order has been re-established, but tension still prevails . . . Kielce is quiet now, but agitators are still spreading rumours that the Jews have killed Poles. A nine-year-old boy who spread the rumour of his alleged detention by Jews is now reported to have said that he was ordered to say so by persons whose names he has given to the police. Forty-six wounded people, some in serious condition, are in hospital. (*The Times*, 6 July 1946)

Many of these people made their way to the Displaced Persons' Camps which were administered by the United Nations in Germany and other countries in Western Europe. Most wanted to emigrate to Palestine:

> The first and plainest need of these people is a recognition of their status as Jews. Refusal to recognise the Jews as such has the effect of closing one's eyes to their former persecution . . . For reasons that are obvious most Jews want to leave Germany and Austria. The life which they have led makes them impatient of delay. They want to be evacuated to Palestine now . . . In conclusion . . . the only real solution of the problem lies in the evacuation of all non-repatriable Jews in Germany and Austria who wish it to Palestine. (Report of Earl G. Harrison to President Truman on the needs of displaced persons in Germany, 1945)

Once the State of Israel had been created, about two-thirds of these displaced Jews settled there. However, Israel would not take the 'chronically sick' and others preferred to go to the United States, Canada or Australia:

> After the war, well it's a long story because I got sick. I had to wait in hospital. I spent over five years in hospitals. It was a tragedy; all my family went to Palestine, but I wasn't well enough. As a matter of fact, I have seven surviving families, brother and sister families in Israel today. When I got better Israel wouldn't take us because we were called the Hard-Core Sick. So I went to America instead of Palestine. (Lavinia and Dan Cohn-Sherbok, *The American Jew*)

The third largest Jewish community after those of the United States and Israel is that of the former Soviet Union. There Jewishness is regarded as a nationality and is stamped in the individual's internal passport. In the post-war period Russian Jews were increasingly subject to discrimination:

I must tell you about Russian anti-Semitism . . . When I was in the East, I heard terrible stories about how Jews kill children and take their blood for Passover bread . . . When we returned to Moscow, my friends helped me to find a job pretty fast, but no one could help my husband. He was a physician, but he couldn't get a job for nine months only because he was a Jew . . . I was a physician at Moscow University . . . I knew the University policies. It was so anti-Semitic you cannot imagine . . . I checked the health of future students. From the 1960s, they stopped taking any Jew to learn law. Nothing, not one Jew. Only 1.5 per cent of all students could be Jews. Every day they checked how many Jewish young people were applying. They used to give me files of students and tell me, 'This student is a sick man – try to find something wrong with him.' (Ibid.)

During the 1950s even the United States was not free from anti-Jewish discrimination in matters of housing and social club membership:

I think the first time that I considered myself strongly as a Jew was after we moved here . . . The representative of an insurance company also represented a real estate development which had a policy of barring Jews from their property. When he attempted to sell me insurance, somehow or other my back went up. I told him that when they changed the policy, we would think about discussing with him the question of insurance. That attitude towards Jews has changed subsequently – partly with a nudging from the Supreme Court! Five years after we came out here, a lawyer whom I know supported me for the City University Club. This did have the reputation for not welcoming Jews. He came back to me and reported that he couldn't get me in. This indicated the somewhat social anti-Semitism that existed in those days. (Ibid.)

Suggested Further Reading

E. Fackenheim, *God's Presence in History: Jewish Affirmations and Philosophical Reflections*, New York: HarperTorchbooks, 1973.

M. Gilbert, *The Holocaust*, London: Collins, 1986.

D. Ben-Gurion, *Israel: The Years of Challenge*, London: Blond, 1963.

A. Hitler, *Mein Kampf*, trans. R. Manheim, Boston: Houghton Mifflin, 1973.

Chronological Table

Circa CE	Documents	Events in Jewish History
1920–30	Hitler's *Mein Kampf*	
1930–40	Nuremberg laws; Party Tribunal report; report in *Völkischer Beobachter*; Peel Commission	Nuremburg laws Kristallnacht
1940–50	Nuremberg laws; Kristallnacht, Alderney interrogation report; Wannsee Conference document; Biltmore Program; Churchill's speech; *The Times* articles; Gromyko's speech; Lestschinsky's *Crisis*; Harrison report	The Final Solution Creation of the State of Israel The War of Independence
1950–60	Kolitz's *Yossel Rakover*	The Suez Crisis
1960–70	Kaplan's *Scroll*; Maybaum's *Face of God*; Rubenstein's *After Auschwitz*; Ben-Gurion's *Israel*	The Six Day War
1970–80	Fackenheim's *God's Presence in History*; Berkovits's *Faith after the Holocaust*; Knesset law; *Encyclopaedia Judaica*	The Yom Kippur War Jerusalem proclaimed capital of Israel
1980–90	Fackenheim's 'On the Jewish People'; Cohn-Sherbok's *Holocaust Theology*; Rubenstein and Roth's *Approaches to Auschwitz*; Gilbert's *Holocaust*; Yermia's article	The invasion of Lebanon

13

Problems of the Jewish Community Today

1. The Problem of Jewish Identity

In the past the question of Jewish identity was simple:

> Now therefore if you will obey my voice and keep my covenant, you shall be my own possession among all peoples; for all the earth is mine, and you shall be to me a kingdom of priests and a holy nation. (Exodus 19: 5–6)

Jewish status was inherited from the mother:

> The son of an Israelite woman is called thy son, but the son by a heathen woman is not called thy son. (Mishnah, Kiddushin III)

Alternatively, it was possible to become Jewish through conversion:

> The Rabbis say: Now if someone comes and wants to be a convert, they say to him: Why do you want to be a convert? Don't you know that the Israelites are harried, hounded, persecuted and harassed and that they suffer many troubles? If he replies: I know that and I am not worthy, then they receive him without further argument. (Talmud, Yebamot XLVII)

Since most Jews were Jewish by birth, irrespective of their personal religious beliefs, the question of the status of apostates to other religions was always troubling. According to Jewish law, apostates remain Jews:

> Apostasy cannot be part to his essential nature; it's only an accident like the change of a name or a change of address. He cannot change his essence because he is a Jew . . . This is what our religion teaches us is true. That is what our Sages meant when they said: Even if he has sinned, he is still part of Israel. (Isaac b. Moses Arama, *Akedat Yizhak*)

However, over the centuries many people have been persecuted as Jews even though they were not accepted as such by the community (for example, through having a Jewish father or their parents having converted to Christianity):

> 7 March 1941. Above this group was another category of 'Jews', those who were born into Christianity . . . But the conquerors checked and rechecked and the family secrets were discovered. Maybe Jewish informers who were jealous of these Christians' peaceful existence were involved, or maybe some Pole tipped the Nazis off about the irregularities in the family trees of their co-religionists. At all events, the conquerors began a hunt for these people who originated from the Jewish race and who, in their eyes, were considered Jewish in every respect. The Nazis brought a caravan of them to the ghetto. (Chaim A. Kaplan, *Scroll of Agony*)

Similarly in the Soviet Union, people were classified by the government as Jews if their fathers were Jews, however tenuous their connection with Judaism:

> In 1971 I went on a business trip to Leningrad where I met my husband . . . He was Jewish, but very different Jewish from my family. I don't think they had done anything in their lives to maintain the Jewish culture. My husband's family had no idea. His father was a member of the Communist party – a big shot at the time . . . We lived with my parents-in-law in their apartment in Leningrad. This is where I first came across anti-Semitism. I couldn't find a job. I went for the first year knocking at every door. They always had to see my passport and once they knew I was Jewish, there was no job. (Lavinia and Dan Cohn-Sherbok, *The American Jew*)

Since World War II, there has been a huge increase in the number of Jews marrying non-Jews in Western Europe and the United States. The children of such marriages are not likely to identify as Jews and this causes much consternation, particularly in Orthodox circles:

> The single most dramatic change in recent years has been in outmarriage itself . . . The turning point came in the 1960s. In the first half of that decade, the rate of intermarriage jumped to 17.4 per cent and by 1971 it had risen to 31.7 per cent. Even then, however, the nature of what was happening was not fully appreciated and it took the 1990 National Jewish Population Survey to send shock waves through American Jewry. What the survey showed was that the rate had risen to 57 per cent. More than one Jew in two was marrying out . . . These are the facts and they are very bad news. In the century of the Holocaust, they are nothing short of tragic. (Jonathan Sacks, *Will We Have Jewish Grandchildren?*)

The Reform Movement (see Chapter 10, Parts 3 and 4) has tried to solve the problem by producing a new definition of Jewishness:

> The Central Conference of American Rabbis declares that the child of one Jewish parent is under the presumption of Jewish descent. The presumption of the Jewish status of the offspring of any mixed marriage is to be established through appropriate and timely public and formal acts of identification with the Jewish faith and people. (Resolution of the Central Conference of American Rabbis, 1983)

The Orthodox, who had never in any case accepted Reform conversion, were appalled by this decision:

> More even than in the case of divorce, the numerical impact of these policies [the Reform policy on conversion and patrilineal descent] is vast. The tragic potential too is immense, for it means that by now some hundreds of thousands of individuals who have received Reform conversions or patrilineal Jewish identity, or are the children of women who have, considered themselves Jewish and halakhically [according to Jewish Law] are not. It is over Reform policies on personal status more than on any other that religious schism threatens Jewry. (Jonathan Sacks, *One People?*)

The situation becomes still more complicated in view of the Law of Return in Israel. Anyone who has a Jewish mother or who has been converted by any branch of Judaism is entitled to immigrate to Israel. Marriage and divorce, on the other hand, is conducted according to Orthodox religious law. This means that Reform converts, many of their children, many ex-Soviet Jews and any other immigrant of 'doubtful origin' may not marry or divorce in Israel, even if they are legitimate Israeli citizens:

> Every Jew has the right to come to this country as an immigrant . . . For the purposes of this law, a 'Jew' means a person who was born of a Jewish mother or has become converted to Judaism and is not a member of another religion. (Israel, The Law of Return 1950/ 1970)

> Matters of marriage and divorce of Jews in Israel, being nationals or residents of the State, shall be under the exclusive jurisdiction of the rabbinical courts. Marriages and divorces of Jews shall be performed in Israel in accordance with Jewish religious law. (Israel, The Rabbinical Courts Jurisdiction (Marriage and Divorce) Law (1953))

2. Divisions within the Diaspora Community

Today the United States has the largest Jewish community in the world:

Only 47 per cent of the Jewish population are affiliated to synagogues. 23 per cent of Jewish households belong to a Conservative congregation. The Conservative movement has a total membership of 1,500,000 and has 830 congregations affiliated to its umbrella organization, the United Synagogue, plus another 100 not affiliated. 13 per cent of households belong to the Reform movement, whose approximately 750 congregations (linked to the Union of American Hebrew Congregations) include 1,100,000 members. 9 per cent belong to one of the 2,500 Orthodox congregations, most of which are affiliated to the Union of Orthodox Jewish Congregations of America. Other Orthodox groupings, including Hasidic groups and the Lubavitch movement, are not affiliated to the UOJCA . . . Unlike other large diaspora communities, such as France and Britain, there is no overall religious leader and no Chief Rabbi . . . Each of the main streams of American Judaism has its own rabbinical association. (Antony Lerman, ed., *The Jewish Communities of the World*)

From the above it will be seen that more than half American Jewry is not affiliated to any synagogue at all and there is serious division among those who do affiliate. Exploring each religious movement in turn:

Those who identified with Conservative Judaism affirmed the end of the ghettoization of the Jews and their emancipation, and the separation of Church and State, as positive goods; they hailed the Westernization of Jews in manner, education and culture; they knew therefore that some changes were inevitable in the modes of Jewish religious life, and they affirmed that these changes could be made validly in the light of biblical and rabbinic precedent, for they viewed the entire history of Judaism as such a succession of changes. They laid the emphasis on Jewish people throughout history as an organism which refreshed its living spirit by responding creatively to new challenges. The founders of Conservative Judaism faced the contemporary age in the belief that the traditional forms and precepts of Judaism were valid and that changes in practice were to be made only with great reluctance. (Arthur Hertzberg, 'Conservative Judaism', *Encyclopaedia Judaica*)

Reform Judaism does more than tolerate diversity, it engenders it . . . We stand open to any position thoughtfully and conscientiously advocated in the spirit of Reform Jewish beliefs. While we may differ in our interpretations and applications of the ideas enunciated here, we accept such differences as precious and see in them Judaism's best hope for confronting whatever the future holds for us . . . The Jewish people and Judaism defy precise definition because both are in the process of becoming Jews by birth or con-

version and so constitute an uncommon union of faith and peoplehood . . .
The Torah [law] results from the relationship between God and the Jewish people . . . Reform Jews are called upon to confront the claims of Jewish tradition, however differently renewed, and to exercise their individual autonomy,
choosing and creating on the basis of commitment and knowledge. (Central
Conference of American Rabbis, The San Francisco Platform, 1976)

In the United States, Orthodoxy constituted one of the mainstreams of
life and thought within Jewry. Different varieties of Orthodoxy coexist-
ed. In 1898 the Union of Orthodox Jewish Congregations of America
was founded. Its declared aims were to accept 'the authoritative interpretation of our rabbis as contained in the Talmud and Codes' . . . The
differences within American Orthodoxy were evidenced by the establishment of different rabbinic bodies there. Rabbis from Eastern Europe,
representing traditional Orthodoxy, made up the Union of Orthodox
Rabbis of the United States and Canada (founded in 1902) while rabbis
educated in America united to form the Rabbinical Council of America
(in 1923: reorganised in 1935). Hasidic groups, who became influential
chiefly after World War II, constitute a separate division within American
Orthodoxy. (Nathaniel Katzburg, 'Orthodoxy', *Encyclopaedia Judaica*)

Unique to the United States is reconstructionism, a movement founded
by Mordecai Kaplan, which grew out of Conservative Judaism. While
retaining the ritual and ethical teaching of Judaism, Kaplan sought to rein-
terpret its theology into non-supernatural terms:

When religion speaks of salvation, it means, in essence, the experience
of the worthwhileness of life. (M. Kaplan, 'The Meaning of God for the
Contemporary Jew', in *Tradition and Contemporary Experience*, ed. A.
Jospe)

God is the sum of all the animating forces and relationships which are for-
ever making a cosmos out of chaos. (M. Kaplan, *The Meaning of God in
Modern Jewish Religion*)

The situation in Great Britain is somewhat different from that of the
United States:

The major body is the United Synagogue which appoints the Chief Rabbi
and maintains his office and the Beth Din [rabbinical court]. The United
Synagogue is Orthodox as are the large majority of synagogues in the
London area . . . The United Synagogue is generally regarded as the 'established' synagogue. More Orthodox is the Federation of Synagogues . . . Even
more Orthodox is the Union of Orthodox Hebrew Congregations. These
two right-wing Orthodox groups together cover 3.5 per cent of the popu-

lation. On the other wing are the Reform Synagogues of Great Britain (13.1 per cent) and the Union of Liberal and Progressive Synagogues (7.1 per cent) . . . The Anglo-Jewish community has the highest level of synagogue affiliation in the Diaspora (85 per cent) and of Orthodox membership (about 80 per cent). (Antony Lerman, ed., *The Jewish Communities of the World*)

Despite these encouraging figures, internal dissension, indifference and assimilation are as much a threat to the British community as to the American. As the Chief Rabbi of the United Synagogues of Great Britain put it:

With a speed and suddenness which has caught us unawares, the chain of Jewish continuity is breaking. In Britain, America and throughout most of the Diaspora, one young Jew in two is deciding not to marry another Jew and have Jewish children. I tremble as I write these words . . . As I have noted already, British Jewry, estimated at 450,000 in the 1950s, is today reduced to number some 300,000. This represents a loss of more than ten Jews a day for forty years. Of these, at most, a fifth have left for Israel. The rest have disaffiliated and disappeared from the Jewish map. (Jonathan Sacks, *Will We Have Jewish Grandchildren?*)

3. The Survival of the State of Israel

Today the only contact of many Jews with their co-religionists is to be found in their support for the State of Israel:

I think Israel is the only thing that affects a lot of Jews, that reminds them that they are Jews. It is quite discouraging the way the trend is towards not being observant and not being involved in Jewish life. There are so many Jewish people in Metropolis who are just sort of in the background. They don't identify as Jews and they don't live as Jews, and they don't support Jewish causes. It's just at crisis times, or when they run into anti-Semitism, that people really get thinking what they should be doing. (Lavinia and Dan Cohn-Sherbok, *The American Jew*)

After the United Nations' vote for the partition of Palestine (see Chapter 12, Part 3), Israel was in effect in a state of siege:

We are concerned with the plain fact that a number of Palestine's neighbour states have sent their troops into Palestine. Our knowledge of the fact is not based on rumours, or newspaper reports, but on official documents signed by the governments of those states informing the Security Council that their troops have entered Palestine . . . I should like to point out in passing that none of the states whose troops have entered Palestine can claim that Palestine

forms part of its territory. (Speech of Soviet delegate Tarasenko to the UN
Security Council, 20 May 1948)

War broke out again in 1956 and 1967. After the Six Day War of 1967,
the United Nations' Security Council passed Resolution 242:

1. The Security Council affirms (a) withdrawal of Israeli armed forces from
territories occupied in the recent conflict. (b) termination of all claims or
states of belligerency and respect for and acknowledgement of the sovereignty, territorial integrity and political independence of every State in the
area and their right to live in peace within secure and recognised boundaries free from threats or acts of force.
2. Affirms further the necessity (a) for guaranteeing freedom of navigation
through international waterways in the area; (b) for achieving a just settlement of the refugee problem; (c) for guaranteeing the territorial inviolabil-
ity and political independence of every State in the area. (UN Security
Council Resolution 242, 22 November 1967)

Although all parties to the conflict accepted the resolution, they did
not agree about its exact meaning and war broke out again in 1973.
Jewish opinion in the Diaspora was galvanized still further by Yassir
Arafat, the leader of the Palestinian Liberation Organization being
invited to speak to the United Nations in 1974 and the resolution of
the following year:

ZIONISM CONDEMNED AT UN. The United Nations General
Assembly tonight adopted a resolution which declared Zionism to be
a 'form of racism and racial discrimination'. The voting was 72 votes
in favour, 35 against and 32 abstentions. (*The Times*, 11 November
1975)

A major step for peace was achieved when President Sadat of Egypt visited Israel in November 1977 and later a treaty was signed between the
two nations:

In the name of God, the Gracious and Merciful. Mr Speaker, Ladies and
Gentlemen . . . I come to you today on solid ground, to shape a new life,
to establish peace. We all, on this land – the land of God, we all, Muslims,
Christians and Jews, worship God and no one but God. God's teachings and
commandments are love, sincerity, purity and peace . . . I have come to you
so that together we might build a durable peace based on justice, to avoid
the shedding of one single drop of blood from an Arab or an Israeli. It is for
this reason I have proclaimed my readiness to go to the furthest corner of
the world . . . You want to live with us in this part of the world. In all sin-

cerity, I tell you, we welcome you among us with full security and safety. (Speech of President Sadat to the Israeli Knesset, 20 November 1977)

The balance was again upset by the Israeli invasion of Lebanon in 1982, officially to root out Palestinian Liberation Organization bases. Even committed Zionists were confused:

ISRAEL ERUPTS . . . Is Israel willing to live in peace with the Palestinians as a people, according to them the same rights that she rightly and insistently demands for herself? Is she willing to liberate Lebanon from the Palestinian burden which is destroying it, not by a war against all Palestinians in Lebanon, but by seeking to accommodate them within Palestine, even if that means giving up part of the historic 'Land of Israel'? (Leading article, *The Times*, 8 June 1982)

The Palestinian intifada (resistance) which began in 1987 has demonstrated that occupying the West Bank and the Gaza strip will be a perpetual problem for the Israelis:

Some 30 per cent of Israeli Jews are willing to grant the essential prerequisite for a Palestinian state: negotiations, substantial territorial concessions and recognition. If questions are worded to make evident that security and peace might be obtained in exchange for these concessions, the favourable proportion increases substantially to 50 per cent or more. (Findings of Professor Elihu Katz in a poll conducted in January 1989)

The recent acceptance of a degree of Palestinian autonomy has been widely welcomed. In any event, despite their interest in and concern for Israeli affairs, the majority of world Jewry will continue to make its home in the Diaspora:

We are privileged to live in an extraordinary time, one in which a third Jewish commonwealth has been established in our people's ancient homeland. We are bound to that land and to the newly reborn State of Israel by innumerable religious and ethnic ties . . . We have both a stake and a responsibility in building the State of Israel, assuring its security and defining its Jewish character. We encourage aliyah [emigration] for those who wish to find maximum personal fulfilment in the cause of Zion . . . At the same time we consider the State of Israel vital to the welfare of Judaism everywhere, we reaffirm the mandate of our tradition to create strong Jewish communities wherever we live. A genuine Jewish life is possible in any land, each community developing its own particular character and determining its Jewish responsibilities. (Central Conference of American Rabbis, The San Francisco Platform, 1976)

4. Rescuing Threatened Communities

After the creation of the State of Israel, the Jewish population of the land grew very rapidly:

Numbers of Jews Living in Palestine

1914	1939	1948	1967	1989
0.1	0.4	0.6	2.4	3.5

(Based on J. Lestschinsky, *Crisis, Catastrophe and Survival*; and *Encyclopaedia Judaica*)

Immigrants arrived not only from the Displaced Persons' Camps of Europe, but also from such ancient communities as those of Iraq (Babylon), Syria and Lebanon:

> The Jews in Turkey are a meagre remnant of once flourishing communities . . . After Israeli independence there was a sudden and unexpected exodus: more than 30,000 Jews left the country in the first two years and the flow has continued. It is reckoned that there are now only 20,000 Jews left in Turkey.
>
> By the time of Israeli independence in 1948, the position of the Jews of Iraq had become untenable and they emigrated en masse leaving their possessions behind them. In 1947 there were thought to have been about 150,000 Jews; by 1952 only some 6,000 remained.
>
> In Syria . . . in the early years of independence there were serious riots which became even more savage after the Israeli War of Independence. Many Jews escaped at considerable risk, and by the mid 1950s the community was reduced to a few thousand.
>
> In Lebanon no anti-Jewish violence was reported during the successive wars with Israel or the internecine fighting which has bedevilled the country since 1975, but economic disruption caused many people to emigrate and there are now only a few hundred Jews left.
>
> There are no reliable statistics for the Jews of Iran. Since the Islamic revolution of 1979 the status of Jews . . . has deteriorated sharply. Hundreds of Jews have been arrested and imprisoned and several were executed for alleged economic crimes or for being 'Zionist spies'. The majority have now fled the country.
>
> In the course of the early Muslim centuries, Jews were gradually eliminated from the Arabian peninsula, except for the Yemen . . . Here thousands of Jews remained in conditions of indescribable deprivation and humiliation . . . In 1949/50, 44,000 Yemenis and 3,000 Adenis were dramatically air-

lifted to Israel in what was called 'Operation Magic Carpet'. Several thousand more left in subsequent years, and it is thought that only a few hundred now remain. (Nicholas de Lange, *Atlas of the Jewish World*)

A similar pattern has appeared in North Africa:

According to the 1947 census there were 203,800 Jews in French Morocco [who] were almost completely despised and hated by the Muslim majority. Soon after the establishment of Israel in 1948, a mass exodus began . . . There are no fewer than 20,000 Jews left in Morocco . . . This is the largest Jewish population in any Arab country and the King has repeatedly expressed his desire to see the Jews live in security and prosperity . . .

Under French rule the Jews of Algeria . . . enjoyed considerable freedom . . . The creation of the State of Israel made little impact here; it was the struggle for independence from France which brought about the liquidation of the ancient community. Caught in a conflict of loyalty to France and to Algeria, the Jews found themselves in an impossible position and they joined the precipitate mass exodus which preceded independence in 1962. 115,000 Algerian Jews arrived in France within the space of a few months . . .

In the early 1950s the Jewish population of Tunisia was calculated at 105,000 . . . On independence in March 1956 . . . large-scale emigration soon ensued . . . The present Jewish population is variously estimated between 3,500 and 7,000 . . .

The 1931 census recorded 24,500 Jews in Libya . . . In Egypt the establishment of Israel in 1948 brought mob violence and official harassment and thousands of Jews left. The harassment became more severe after General Abdel Nasser seized power in 1954; following the Suez campaign of 1956 thousands more Jews had their possessions confiscated and were forced to leave the country . . . By 1979 . . . there were only a few hundred Jews remaining in Cairo and Alexandria. (Ibid.)

The community that has captured the imagination of the world is that of the black Jews of Ethiopia. In 1973 the Sephardi Chief Rabbi pronounced that they really were Jews and two years later they were declared eligible for Israeli citizenship under the Law of Return. In 1984 many thousands were airlifted from famine-ridden Ethiopia to a new life:

SECRET AIRLIFT OF ETHIOPIA'S JEWISH COMMUNITY. MODERN EXODUS OF THE LOST TRIBE OF ISRAEL. Israel has been masterminding a secret air-lift from drought-stricken Africa in the last two months which officials claim has brought thousands of Ethiopian Jews to Israel as new immigrants, many of them crippled by tropical diseases and the effects of severe malnutrition. Although exact figures have not been provided, the news blackout surrounding the operation was broken after Mr Yehuda

Dominits, chief of the Jewish Agency's immigration department, disclosed that most of Ethiopia's 25,000 strong community – known locally as Falashas – was now in Israel. (*The Times*, 4 January 1985)

The rescue of Soviet Jewry, the third largest community in the world, has been another preoccupation:

I was born in the Soviet Union, in the suburbs of Moscow. I consider myself a bit different from the majority of Russian Jews because I received a Jewish education and upbringing in Russia. It was underground, which means nobody knew about it. In some ways I can say I was leading two lives; outside in school and on the street, I was like everybody else, and at home we observed all the holidays and traditions . . . When we had a chance to leave Russia, we were one of the first to apply, and we was denied the visa for three years but then we were able to leave Russia for Israel. (Lavinia and Dan Cohn-Sherbok, *The American Jew*)

The campaign for Soviet Jewry was presented as an issue of religious freedom. In fact many of the emigrants wanted to escape the economic constraints of the Soviet system:

At those times everyone was leaving Russia with Israeli visas. Then what happened was that they would come to Vienna and say, 'We don't want to go to Israel. We want to go to America.' . . . I would say they didn't want to go to Israel mainly because of the war. Russian Jews suffered in the Second World War and they had many relatives who were killed . . . You must understand, in the 1970s, people who were close to the Zionist idea were going to Israel. People who were leaving for economic reasons, they wanted to go to America. (Ibid.)

5. Judaism and Feminism

Judaism is essentially a patriarchal religion with clearly defined roles for men and women. Although Jewishness is passed down through the mother rather than the father, the birth of a baby boy has traditionally been the cause for far more rejoicing than the birth of a baby girl:

My arrival in the world was a disappointment to a number of people and especially to my grandfather, Reb Chaim . . . It was not a boy – only I had come into the world . . . He hated me from the very first for the disappointment and humiliation I had caused him. (Lucy Robins Lang, *Tomorrow is Beautiful*)

The ritual circumcision of the new male child is an excuse for a major celebration. The births of female children are merely recorded by a baby blessing during the course of a normal synagogue service:

> Sociologist Rela Geffen Monson comments that the two events most likely to startle a Jewish woman into an awareness of her inequality in the tradition are the death of a parent – that is, when the mourning woman cannot participate in the communal minyan [worship group of ten men] – and the birth of a daughter when all the people who had planned to come for the circumcision cancel their reservations. (Susan Weidman Schneider, *Jewish and Female*)

Again, at the age of thirteen, the young boy 'becomes a man'; he is publicly and ceremoniously called up to read from the Scrolls of the Law and becomes Bar Mitzvah (son of the commandment). Traditionally there is no parallel service for girls:

> Until this century, the marking of a young person's coming of age in Judaism, the formal recognition of the assumption of adult obligations in the community, belonged only to boys. Bar Mitzvah was the authentic rite of passage into Judaism and girls knew about it only as passive observers . . . Since Orthodox congregations do not allow women to appear on the bimah [synagogue dais] before a mixed congregation, ceremonies marking the coming of age of Orthodox girls are usually held at home . . . In some families there is simply a party to mark the milestone and in some no notice is taken at all. (Ibid.)

Women are exempt from all positive, time-bound commandments and so have no obligation to take part in communal prayer and worship. The different morning blessings for men and women are instructive:

> All say: Blessed art thou O Lord our God, King of the Universe, who hast not made me a heathen. Blessed art thou O Lord our God, King of the Universe who hast not made me a slave.
> Men say: Blessed art thou O Lord our God, King of the Universe, who hast not made me a woman.
> Women say: Blessed art thou O Lord our God, King of the Universe, who hast made me according to thy will. (Authorised Daily Prayer Book)

Traditionally, marriage and motherhood are the only acceptable destinies for Jewish women:

> On the eve of Sabbaths and of Holy days, it is customary for parents either at the conclusion of the service in the synagogue, or upon reaching their home, to proclaim the following benedictions upon their children:

To sons say: God make thee as Ephraim and Manasseh.
To daughters say: God make thee as Sarah, Rebekah, Rachel and Leah.
(Ibid.)

Very little has changed in the Orthodox community:

Still traditional Jews remain avowedly committed to marriage . . . Many factors come into play; traditional notions of marriage are but one part of a much larger system of traditional values . . . In consequence while the average marriage age for women in America has advanced several years during the past decade, Orthodox women still tend to marry in their early twenties. Given a strong commitment to marriage for our children and ourselves, there are a hundred things we can do to broaden the circle of friends of similar backgrounds from which to seek a suitable mate. (Blu Greenberg, *How to Run a Traditional Jewish Household*)

In the non-Orthodox community, things are very different. The complete equality of the sexes has always been an important principle in Reform Judaism:

The participation of women in religious and communal life is indispensable. They should receive their equal share in religious duties as well as rights. (Guidelines for a Programme of Liberal Judaism, 1912)

Consequently new celebrations have been introduced for the birth of daughters and for a girl's coming-of-age ceremony:

Oh boy, it's a girl!!! With the new interest in Jewish feminism, many people have reassessed their needs and values and have written their own brit [covenant] ceremonies. We include some of the many sent to us with the hope that they inspire other parents to explore the tradition and their own Jewish needs. Though to date none have been adopted as accepted ritual by any recognized religious group, this should not prevent anyone from working on his/her own version. Remember that there isn't a lot of time from the birth of the baby to the time of the brit (if you intend to observe the girl's brit on the eighth day), so you might think ahead and consider using biblical passages . . . featuring female heroines (the seven prophetesses: Sarah, Miriam, Deborah, Hannah, Abigail, Huldah, and Esther) or other women of note in the Bible. (Sharon and Michael Strassfeld, *The Second Jewish Catalog*)

However, for many educated women, the Jewish religious vision remains too patriarchal:

I do wonder if the phrase 'a Jewish feminist' is not a contradiction in terms
. . . Many people just step outside and forget about Judaism entirely . . .
Obviously Judaism is a patriarchal religion; obviously it's institutionalized sex-
ism. It's role based; it's gender based. As far as feminists go, I have so much
experience of women starting off exploring their Judaism and ending up
being goddess worshippers. I've seen this trend a lot. I went to this fasci-
nating lecture by someone called Starhawk, who's written several books. She
was born Jewish and she said in her talk that she's a little bit of everything.
And you can see why. She's having a great time; she's banging a drum; she's
the centre of her life. So I ask myself, 'Why this attachment to Judaism?' I
don't particularly want to beat a drum, but figuratively maybe I do want to
beat a drum! (Lavinia and Dan Cohn-Sherbok, *The American Jew*)

Afterword

No Reader in Judaism would be complete without some prayers from the traditional liturgy:

Blessed art thou, Lord our God, King of the Universe, who hast sanctified us with his commandments, and hast commanded us to engage in the study of the words of the divine Law.

Blessed art thou, O Lord our God, King of the Universe, who hast chosen us from among the nations and hast given us his law. Blessed art thou, O God, who hast given us the Law.

May the Lord bless you and keep you. May the Lord let the light of his countenance shine upon you and be gracious unto you. May the Lord shed the light of his countenance upon you and give you peace.

Hear O Israel, the Lord our God, the Lord is One. And you shall love the Lord your God with all your heart, and with all your soul and with all your strength. And these words which I command you this day shall be written on your heart. You shall teach them diligently to your children, and will speak of them when you sit in your house and when you go on your way and when you lie down and when you rise up. And you shall bind them as a sign upon your hand, and they shall be as frontlets between your eyes. And you shall write them up on the doorposts of your house and upon your gates.

Blessed art thou O Lord, our God and God of our fathers, the God of Abraham and the God of Isaac and the God of Jacob, the God who is great, who is mighty and who is tremendous; the most high God, who giveth gracious favours, possessor of all, who remembereth the pious deeds of the Patriarchs, and who bringeth a Redeemer in love to the last generation. King, Helper, Saviour and Shield. Blessed art thou O God, the shield of Abraham.

May he who makes peace in the highest Heavens, grant peace unto us and unto all Israel. And so say Amen.

Hear O Israel, the Lord our God, the Lord is One.

Index of Authors and Works